JELL-O
Easy
Entertaining

Introduction

Everyone loves to serve magnificent desserts when they entertain. Most of us, however, think we have neither the time nor the talent to make them. *Easy Entertaining* with JELL-O offers the perfect solution to both of these problems.

Contained in this incredible recipe collection of over 80 recipes are desserts for any occasion. Not only are these irresistible desserts guaranteed to impress your family and friends alike, but they all offer the added bonus of being super-quick and easy to make.

As an added guarantee of success, we have included a special "Tricks of the Trade" chapter complete with no-fail tips that promise to make each and every luscious dessert as beautiful as it is delicious!

Tricks of the Trade

Our professionals share their secrets with you—simple additions guaranteed to add pizzazz to any recipe. These foolproof tips, many with step-by-step photos, ensure perfect results every time and the quick, clever garnish ideas are sure to impress family and friends alike.

Gelatin

Making JELL-O Brand Gelatin is easy—you've probably been doing it since you were little. Just follow the package directions and the results are terrific!

The basic directions as written below are also on the package:

- Add 1 cup boiling water to 1 package (4-serving size) gelatin (2 cups water for 8-serving size). Stir until dissolved, about 2 minutes. Add 1 cup cold water (2 cups for 8-serving size). Chill until set.

- JELL-O Brand Sugar Free Gelatin is prepared in the same way. It can be used in any recipe that calls for JELL-O Brand Gelatin.

Some tips for success

- To make a mixture that is clear and uniformly set, be sure the gelatin is completely dissolved in boiling water or other boiling liquid before adding the cold liquid.

- To double a recipe, just double the amounts of gelatin, liquid and other ingredients used except salt, vinegar and lemon juice. For these, use just 1½ times the amount given in the recipe.

- To store prepared gelatin overnight or longer, cover it to prevent drying. Always store gelatin cakes or pies in the refrigerator.

How to speed up chilling time

- Choose the *right container*—a metal bowl or mold rather than glass, plastic or china. Metal chills more quickly and the gelatin will be firm in less time than in glass or plastic bowls. Also, individual servings in small molds or serving dishes will chill more quickly than large servings.

- Speed set (ice cube method): Dissolve gelatin completely in ¾ cup boiling liquid (1½ cups for 8-serving size). Combine ½ cup water and enough ice cubes to make 1¼ cups (1 cup cold water and enough ice cubes to make 2½ cups for 8-serving size). Add to gelatin, stirring until slightly thickened. Remove any unmelted ice. Pour into dessert dishes or serving bowl. Chill. Mixture will be soft-set and ready to eat in about 30 minutes, firm in 1 to 1½ hours. However, <u>do not</u> use this method if you are going to mold the gelatin.

Gelatin Chilling Time Chart

In all recipes, for best results, the gelatin needs to be chilled to the proper consistency. Use this chart as a guideline to determine the desired consistency and the approximate chilling time.

When recipe says:	It means gelatin should . . .	It will take about:		Use it for . . .
		Regular set	Speed set*	
"Chill until syrupy"	be consistency of thick syrup	1 hour	3 minutes	glaze for pies, fruits
"Chill until slightly thickened"	be consistency of unbeaten egg whites	1¼ hours	5 to 6 minutes	adding creamy ingredients such as whipped topping, or when mixture will be beaten
"Chill until thickened"	be thick enough so that spoon drawn through it leaves a definite impression	1½ hours	7 to 8 minutes	adding solid ingredients such as fruits or vegetables
"Chill until set but not firm"	stick to the finger when touched and should mound or move to the side when bowl or mold is tilted	2 hours	30 minutes	layering gelatin mixtures
"Chill until firm"	not stick to finger when touched and not mound or move when mold is tilted	Individual molds: at least 3 hours; 2- to 6-cup mold: at least 4 hours; 8- to 12-cup mold: at least 5 hours or overnight		unmolding and serving

*Speed set (ice cube method) not recommended for molding.

- Ice bath method: Dissolve gelatin according to package directions. Place bowl of gelatin mixture in larger bowl of ice and water; stir occasionally as mixture chills to ensure even thickening.

- Blender method: Place 4-serving size package of gelatin and ¾ cup boiling liquid in blender. (Note: The volume of the 8-serving size package is too large for most blenders.) Cover and blend at low speed until gelatin is completely dissolved, about 30 seconds. Combine ½ cup water and enough ice cubes to make 1¼ cups; add to gelatin. Stir until partially melted. Blend at high speed 30 seconds. Pour into dessert dishes or bowl. Chill until set, at least 30 minutes. Mixture is self-layering and sets with a frothy layer on top, clear layer on bottom.

The Secret to Molding Gelatin

The Mold
- Use metal molds, traditional decorative molds and other metal forms, as well. You can use square or round cake pans, fluted or plain tube pans, loaf pans, metal mixing bowls (the nested sets give you a variety of sizes), or metal fruit or juice cans (to unmold, dip can in warm water, then puncture bottom of can and unmold).

- To determine the *volume of the mold,* measure first with water. Most recipes give an indication of the size of the mold needed. For clear gelatin, you need a 2-cup mold for a 4-serving size package of gelatin, and a 4-cup mold for 8-serving size.

- If mold holds less than the amount called for, pour the extra gelatin mixture into a separate dish and serve at another time. Do not use a mold that is too large, since it would be difficult to unmold. Either increase the recipe or use a smaller mold.

- For easier unmolding, spray mold with non-stick cooking spray before filling mold.

The Preparation
- Use less water in preparing gelatin if it is to be molded. For 4-serving size package, use ¾ cup cold water; for 8-serving size, use 1½ cups cold water. (This adjustment has already been made in recipes in this magazine that are to be molded.) This makes the mold less fragile and makes unmolding much simpler.

- To arrange fruits or vegetables in molds, chill gelatin until thick, then pour gelatin into mold to about ¼-inch depth. Arrange fruits or vegetables in decorative pattern in gelatin. Chill until set but not firm, then pour remaining thickened gelatin over pattern in mold.

The Unmolding
- First, allow gelatin to set until firm, several hours or overnight. Also, chill serving plate or individual plates on which mold will be served.

- Make certain that gelatin is completely firm. It should not feel sticky on top and should not mound or move to the side if mold is tilted.

- Moisten tips of fingers and gently pull gelatin from edge of mold. Or, use a small metal spatula or pointed knife dipped in warm water to loosen top edge.

- Dip mold in warm, not hot, water, just to the rim, for about 10 seconds. Lift from water, hold upright and shake to loosen gelatin. Or, gently pull gelatin from edge of mold.

- Moisten chilled serving plate with cold water; this allows gelatin to be moved after unmolding. Place moistened plate over mold and invert. Shake slightly, then lift off mold carefully. If gelatin doesn't release easily, dip the mold in warm water again for a few seconds. If necessary, move gelatin to center of serving plate.

Unmolding Gelatin

1. Before unmolding, pull gelatin from edge of mold with moist fingers. Or, run small metal spatula or pointed knife dipped in warm water around edge of gelatin.

2. Dip mold in warm water, just to rim, for 10 seconds.

3. Lift from water and gently pull gelatin from edge of mold with moist fingers.

4. Place moistened serving plate on top of mold.

5. Invert mold and plate and shake to loosen gelatin.

6. Gently remove mold and center gelatin on plate.

Pudding Pointers

The recipes in this book use both **JELL-O Pudding and Pie Filling**, which requires cooking, and **JELL-O Instant Pudding and Pie Filling**, which is not cooked. These products are not interchangeable in recipes. Be sure to use the product called for in the recipe.

The basic directions as written below are also on the package:

For JELL-O Pudding and Pie Filling:
- Stir contents of 1 package (4-serving size) pudding mix into 2 cups milk (3 cups for 6-serving size) in medium saucepan. Cook and stir over medium heat until mixture comes to full boil. Pudding thickens as it cools. Serve warm or cold.

- Microwave directions: Stir pudding mix with milk in 1½-quart (2-quart for 6-serving size) microwavable bowl. Microwave on HIGH 6 minutes (8 minutes for 6-serving size), stirring every 2 minutes, until mixture comes to boil. Stir well. Chill. Note: Ovens vary; cooking time is approximate. Microwave method not recommended for ovens below 500 watts.

- For pie, cool cooked pudding 5 minutes, stirring twice. Pour into cooled, baked 8-inch pie shell (9-inch highly fluted or 10-inch for 6-serving size). Chill 3 hours.

- JELL-O Lemon Flavor Pie Filling has different directions that call for eggs, sugar and water rather than milk; follow the package directions to make a delicious lemon meringue pie.

For JELL-O Instant Pudding and Pie Filling:
- Pour 2 cups cold milk (3 cups for 6-serving size) into bowl. Add pudding mix. Beat with wire whisk or at lowest speed of electric mixer until well blended, 1 to 2 minutes. Pour immediately into dishes. Pudding will be soft-set, ready to eat in 5 minutes.

- For pies, beat only 1 minute; mixture will be thin. Pour immediately into cooled, baked pie shell (8-inch for 4-serving size, 9-inch for 6-serving size). Chill at least 1 hour. For chocolate, chocolate fudge, milk chocolate or butterscotch flavors, 4-serving size, reduce milk to 1¾ cups; for chocolate and chocolate fudge flavors, 6-serving size, reduce milk to 2⅔ cups.

- Shaker method: Pour cold milk into leakproof 1-quart container (1½-quart container for 6-serving size). Add pudding mix. Cover tightly. Shake vigorously at least 45 seconds. Pour immediately into dessert dishes or serving bowl.

- Fork-Stir method: Place mix in 1-quart bowl. While stirring with fork, gradually add milk. Stir until blended and smooth, about 2 minutes.

- Blender method: Pour cold milk into electric blender. Add pudding mix; cover. Blend at high speed 15 seconds. Pour immediately into dessert dishes or pie shell.

JELL-O Sugar Free Pudding and Pie Filling and Sugar Free Instant Pudding and Pie Filling can be substituted for their respective cooked and instant pudding mixes.

Some tips for success

For JELL-O Pudding and Pie Filling:
- It's best to cook pudding in a heavy saucepan to ensure even heating. Stir pudding mixture constantly as it cooks. Make sure it comes to full boil. The mixture will be thin, but will thicken as it cools.

- For a creamier pudding, stir before serving.

- To cool pudding quickly, place pan of hot pudding in larger pan of ice water; stir frequently until mixture is cooled. Do not use this method for pie filling; the set will not be firm enough.

- For molded pudding recipes, cool cooked pudding 5 minutes, stirring twice; then pour into plain mold or individual custard cups that have been rinsed in cold water. Chill. To unmold, dip mold or cup in hot water.

For JELL-O Instant Pudding and Pie Filling:
- Always use cold milk. Beat pudding mix slowly, not vigorously.

- For best results, use whole or 2% milk. Skim milk, reconstituted nonfat dry milk, light cream or half and half can also be used.

- Always store prepared pudding desserts, snacks and pies in refrigerator.

Pudding Cake Pointers

Adding instant pudding mix to cake mix gives cakes an extra richness and moistness and a homemade taste. For perfect results:

- Follow recipe directions carefully, beating just the time specified and baking at the correct temperature.

- If your cakes usually take less or more time than the time range specified, you might need to have your oven's thermostat checked for accuracy.

- When using a *pudding-included cake mix,* you probably will have to reduce the liquid ingredients. Reduce the water or other liquid by ¼ cup. If sour cream is used rather than water, reduce that by ¼ cup.

- If you're using a different size pan than what is called for in the recipe, the baking time will change. A cake baked in smaller pans—8-inch rather than 9-inch layers, for example—will take slightly longer, 5 to 10 minutes.

- The best tests of doneness: a cake tester inserted in center comes out clean; cake has begun to pull away from sides of pan; or cake springs back when lightly touched.

Show Stoppers

It's those finishing touches that make the professionals' desserts so special. Here are their secrets.

Citrus Twists

1. With sharp knife, cut orange into thin slices.

2. Cut slit through slices to centers.

3. Twist slices from slits in opposite directions to form twists.

Citrus Curls

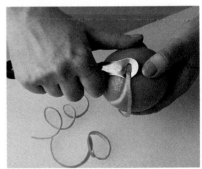

Use citrus zester to remove long thin strip of peel from around lemon, lime or orange. Cut into desired length. Roll strip into curl; use as garnish.

Citrus Zest Strips

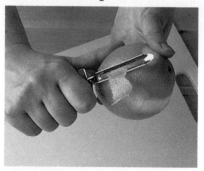

1. *Use vegetable peeler to shave off topmost layer from orange peel in wide strips.*

2. *With sharp knife, cut peel into narrow strips. Use to flavor desserts or as a garnish.*

Tinted Coconut

Dilute a few drops of food coloring with ½ teaspoon milk or water; add 1 to 1⅓ cups coconut. Toss with fork until evenly tinted.

Toasted Coconut

Spread coconut in shallow pan. Toast at 350°, stirring frequently, 7 to 12 minutes or until lightly browned. Or toast in microwave oven on HIGH, 5 minutes for 1⅓ cups, stirring several times.

Citrus Fans

1. *With sharp knife, cut orange into thin slices.*

2. *Stack 3 slices; cut slit through slices to center.*

3. *Twist slices from slits in opposite directions; twist 3 slices together to give fan effect.*

Fruit Fans

1. With sharp knife, cut drained canned pear halves into thin slices (about 5 or 6), cutting up to, but not through, stem ends. (Use same technique for strawberries.)

2. Hold stem end in place and gently fan out slices from stem before placing on plate for fruit desserts or using as garnish.

Frosted Fruit

Use fresh cranberries or green or red seedless grapes. Dip fruit into 1 lightly beaten egg white. (Note: Use only clean eggs with no cracks in shells.) Hold to permit excess egg white to drain off; roll in sugar in flat plate to coat well. Place on tray covered with waxed paper. Let stand until dry.

Whipped Topping Piping

Insert decorating tip in pastry bag; fill with thawed COOL WHIP Whipped Topping. Fold down top of pastry bag. Holding bag firmly with one hand and squeezing topping down into tip, guide tip around surface to be decorated. Double back topping at intervals for decorative wave effect.

Whipped Topping Dollops

1. Swirl spoon, held upright, through thawed COOL WHIP Whipped Topping, creating rippled surface on the topping.

2. Dip spoon into rippled topping to scoop up heaping spoonful of topping, maintaining rippled surface.

3. Gently touch spoon onto surface of dessert and release topping gradually onto surface, pulling spoon up into a crowning tip.

Sauce Swirls

1. Spoon Vanilla Sauce (see page 24 for recipe) onto individual dessert plates. Drop small amounts of sauce (chocolate, raspberry or strawberry) or melted chocolate from spoon at intervals over Vanilla Sauce near rim of plate.

2. Draw wooden pick through sauce, swirling through Vanilla Sauce to create design.

Toasted Nuts

Spread nuts in shallow baking pan. Toast at 400°, stirring frequently, 8 to 10 minutes or until golden brown.

Gumdrop Ribbon

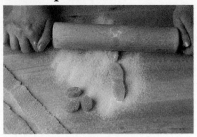

1. Line up gumdrops in a row on surface or sheet of waxed paper sprinkled with sugar. Flatten into long strips with rolling pin, turning frequently to coat with sugar.

2. Cut flattened gumdrops with sharp knife into 1-inch strips.

3. To make bow, fold over four strips to form loops of the bow; place on dessert. Then place a small loop in center to cover center of bow. Cut "V"'s at one end of remaining two strips, if desired; place under loops to resemble ends of ribbon.

Gumdrop Flowers

1. Flatten gumdrops with rolling pin on surface or sheet of waxed paper sprinkled with sugar. Roll until very thin (about ⅟₁₆ inch thick), turning frequently to coat with sugar.

2. Hold flattened gumdrop at center; overlap edges slightly to give petal effect, pressing piece together at base to resemble flower. For open blossom, bend gumdrop petals outward from center. Insert small piece of gumdrop in centers with wooden pick, if desired. Use wooden pick to attach flowers to cake if necessary.

Easy Chocolate Garnishes

Use BAKER'S Semi-Sweet or GERMAN'S Sweet Chocolate.

To melt on range top: Place chocolate in heavy saucepan over *very low* heat; stir *constantly* until just melted.

To melt Semi-Sweet Chocolate in microwave: Place 1 square chocolate, unwrapped, in microwavable dish. Microwave on HIGH 1 to 2 minutes or until almost melted, stirring halfway through heating time. Remove from oven; stir until completely melted. Add 10 seconds for each additional square of chocolate.

To melt GERMAN'S Sweet Chocolate in microwave: Place chocolate, unwrapped and broken in half, in microwavable dish. Microwave on HIGH 1½ to 2 minutes until almost melted, stirring halfway through heating time. Remove from oven; stir until completely melted.

2. To make curls, slip tip of straight-side metal spatula under chocolate. Push spatula firmly along baking sheet, under chocolate, so chocolate curls as it is pushed. (If chocolate is too firm to curl, let stand a few minutes at room temperature; chill again if it becomes too soft.)

3. Carefully pick up each chocolate curl by inserting wooden pick in center. Lift onto waxed paper-lined baking sheet. Chill until firm, about 15 minutes. Arrange on desserts. (Lift with wooden pick to prevent breakage or melting.)

Chocolate Curls

1. Spread 4 squares melted chocolate with spatula into very thin layer on baking sheet. Chill until firm but still pliable, about 10 minutes.

Chocolate Cutouts

1. Pour melted chocolate onto waxed paper-lined baking sheet; spread to 1/8-inch thickness with spatula. Chill until firm, about 15 minutes.

2. Cut with cookie cutters; immediately lift gently from waxed paper with spatula or knife. Store on waxed paper in refrigerator or freezer. Use to garnish desserts.

Chocolate-Dipped Garnish

Dip fruit, cookies or whole nuts into melted chocolate, covering at least half; let excess chocolate drip off. Arrange on rack or place on waxed paper-lined tray. Let stand or chill until chocolate is firm.

Chocolate Drizzle

1. Place 1 square BAKER'S Semi-Sweet Chocolate in small plastic sandwich bag or self-closing bag. Microwave on HIGH about 1 minute or until chocolate is melted. Fold top of bag tightly and snip off one corner (about 1/8 inch).

2. Hold bag tightly at top and drizzle chocolate through opening over fruit, cookies, cake or pudding.

Shaved Chocolate

Pull vegetable peeler across surface of chocolate square, using short, quick strokes. Sprinkle the shaved chocolate on beverages or desserts.

Quick and Easy

Black Forest Parfaits

1 package (8 ounces)
    PHILADELPHIA BRAND
    Cream Cheese, softened
2 cups cold milk
1 package (4-serving size)
    JELL-O Instant Pudding
    and Pie Filling, Chocolate
    Flavor
1 can (21 ounces) cherry pie
    filling
1 tablespoon cherry liqueur
½ cup chocolate wafer crumbs

BEAT cream cheese with ½ cup of
the milk at low speed of electric
mixer until smooth. Add pudding
mix and remaining milk. Beat until
smooth, 1 to 2 minutes.

MIX together cherry pie filling and
liqueur. Reserve a few cherries for
garnish, if desired. Spoon ½ of the
pudding mixture evenly into
individual dessert dishes; sprinkle
with wafer crumbs. Cover with pie
filling; top with remaining
pudding mixture. Chill until ready
to serve. Garnish with reserved
cherries and additional wafer
crumbs, if desired.

MAKES 4 to 6 servings

Prep time: 15 minutes

Creamy Orange Pie

1 package (4-serving size)
    JELL-O Brand Gelatin,
    Orange Flavor
1 cup boiling water
1 pint vanilla ice cream,
    softened
1 packaged chocolate crumb
    crust
    COOL WHIP Whipped
    Topping, thawed

DISSOLVE gelatin in boiling water.
Spoon in ice cream, stirring until
melted and smooth. Chill until
slightly thickened, about 10
minutes.

POUR gelatin mixture into crust.
Chill until firm, about 2 hours.
Garnish with whipped topping.

MAKES 8 servings

Prep time: 15 minutes
Chill time: 2 hours

Black Forest Parfaits

Trifle Cups

1 package (4-serving size)
   JELL-O Brand Gelatin,
   Raspberry Flavor
¾ cup boiling water
1 package (10 ounces) BIRDS
   EYE Quick Thaw Red
   Raspberries, thawed
   Ice cubes
12 shortbread or sugar cookies
1½ cups cold half and half or
   milk
1 package (4-serving size)
   JELL-O Instant Pudding
   and Pie Filling, French
   Vanilla or Vanilla Flavor
½ cup thawed COOL WHIP
   Whipped Topping

DISSOLVE gelatin in boiling water.
Drain raspberries, reserving syrup.
Combine syrup and ice cubes to
make 1 cup. Add to gelatin, stirring
until ice is melted. Place bowl in
larger bowl of ice and water. Let
stand, stirring occasionally, until
gelatin is slightly thickened, about
5 minutes. Reserve 6 raspberries
for garnish, if desired. Stir
remaining raspberries into gelatin.

CRUMBLE cookies into individual
dessert dishes. Spoon gelatin
mixture over cookies; chill until
set but not firm.

POUR half and half into small
bowl. Add pudding mix. Beat with
wire whisk until well blended,
about 1 to 2 minutes. Let stand 5
minutes or until slightly thickened.
Fold in whipped topping. Spoon
over gelatin mixture. Chill until

set, about 1 hour. Garnish with
reserved raspberries and additional
whipped topping, if desired.
           MAKES 6 servings

Prep time: 20 minutes
Chill time: 1 hour

Pinwheel Cake and Cream

*A quick and easy dessert to make
with any fruit.*

1 package (4-serving size)
   JELL-O Instant Pudding
   and Pie Filling, French
   Vanilla or Vanilla Flavor
2 cups cold milk
1 cup thawed COOL WHIP
   Whipped Topping
1 teaspoon grated orange
   rind
1 small peach or nectarine,
   cut into bite-size pieces
1 pound cake loaf (about
   12 ounces), cut into slices
2 cups summer fruit*

PREPARE pudding mix with milk
as directed on package. Let stand 5
minutes or until slightly thickened.
Fold in whipped topping, orange
rind and peach.

ARRANGE pound cake slices on
serving plate. Spoon pudding
mixture evenly over center of cake
slices. Arrange fruit in pudding
mixture. Chill until ready to serve.
           MAKES 10 servings

*We suggest any variety of berries,
seedless grapes or sliced peaches,
nectarines or plums.

Prep time: 15 minutes

Pinwheel Cake and Cream

Ice Cream Shop Pie ∿

Cool, fun and delicious!

1½ cups cold half and half or
    milk
1 package (4-serving size)
    JELL-O Instant Pudding
    and Pie Filling, any flavor
3½ cups (8 ounces) COOL WHIP
    Whipped Topping, thawed
    Ice Cream Shop Ingredients*
1 packaged chocolate,
    graham cracker or vanilla
    crumb crust

POUR half and half into large
bowl. Add pudding mix. Beat with
wire whisk until well blended, 1 to
2 minutes. Let stand 5 minutes or
until slightly thickened.

FOLD whipped topping and Ice
Cream Shop Ingredients into
pudding mixture. Spoon into crust.

FREEZE pie until firm, about 6
hours or overnight. Remove from
freezer. Let stand at room
temperature about 10 minutes
before serving to soften. Store any
leftover pie in freezer.

MAKES 8 servings

Rocky Road Pie: Use any
chocolate flavor pudding mix and
chocolate crumb crust. Fold in ½
cup *each* BAKER'S Semi-Sweet Real
Chocolate Chips, KRAFT Miniature
Marshmallows and chopped nuts
with whipped topping. Serve with
chocolate sauce, if desired.

Toffee Bar Crunch Pie: Use
French vanilla or vanilla flavor
pudding mix and graham cracker
crumb crust, spreading ⅓ cup
butterscotch sauce onto bottom of
crust before filling. Fold in 1 cup
chopped chocolate-covered

English toffee bars (about 6 bars)
with whipped topping. Garnish
with additional chopped toffee
bars, if desired.

Strawberry Banana Split Pie:
Use French vanilla or vanilla flavor
pudding mix, reducing half and
half to ¾ cup and adding ¾ cup
pureed BIRDS EYE Quick Thaw
Strawberries with the half and half.
Use vanilla crumb crust and line
bottom with banana slices. Garnish
with whipped topping, maraschino
cherries and chopped nuts. Serve
with remaining strawberries,
pureed, if desired.

Chocolate Cookie Pie: Use
French vanilla or vanilla flavor
pudding mix and chocolate crumb
crust. Fold in 1 cup chopped
chocolate sandwich cookies with
whipped topping.

Nutcracker Pie: Use butter pecan
flavor pudding mix and graham
cracker crumb crust. Fold in 1 cup
chopped mixed nuts with whipped
topping.

Peppermint Stick Pie: Use French
vanilla or vanilla flavor pudding
mix and chocolate crumb crust.
Fold in ½ cup crushed hard
peppermint candies, ½ cup
BAKER'S Semi-Sweet Real
Chocolate Chips and 2 teaspoons
peppermint extract with whipped
topping.

Prep time: 15 minutes
Freezing time: 6 hours

*Top to bottom: Rocky Road Pie;
Toffee Bar Crunch Pie; Strawberry
Banana Split Pie*

Cappuccino Cups

The coffee and cinnamon in this recipe make a wonderful flavor combination.

12 chocolate wafer cookies
4 teaspoons instant espresso powder*
1 tablespoon hot water
1½ cups cold half and half or milk
1 package (4-serving size) JELL-O Instant Pudding and Pie Filling, French Vanilla or Vanilla Flavor
½ teaspoon ground cinnamon
3½ cups (8 ounces) COOL WHIP Whipped Topping, thawed
1 jar (11.4 ounces) hot fudge sauce
2 to 4 tablespoons coffee liqueur (optional)
Chocolate-covered espresso beans for garnish (optional)

PLACE 1 cookie in each of 12 muffin cups, trimming to fit, if necessary.

DISSOLVE espresso powder in hot water in medium bowl. Add half and half, pudding mix and cinnamon. Beat with wire whisk until well blended, 1 to 2 minutes. Let stand 5 minutes or until slightly thickened. Fold in whipped topping. Spoon into muffin cups. Freeze until firm, about 6 hours.

HEAT fudge sauce with liqueur just before serving; keep warm. Run thin knife around rim of each muffin cup; remove dessert. Place on individual dessert plate. (If frozen solid, let stand 5 minutes to soften slightly.)

Top: Cappuccino Cups; bottom: Chocolate Orange Cream

SPOON sauce around each dessert. Garnish with additional whipped topping, cinnamon and chocolate-covered espresso beans, if desired.
MAKES 12 servings

*2 tablespoons instant coffee powder may be substituted for the espresso powder.

Prep time: 15 minutes
Freezing time: 6 hours

Chocolate Orange Cream

Super easy and super delicious!

½ cup cold milk
½ cup cold orange juice
1 to 2 tablespoons orange liqueur or orange juice
1 package (4-serving size) JELL-O Instant Pudding and Pie Filling, Chocolate Flavor
1¾ cups (4 ounces) COOL WHIP Whipped Topping, thawed
5 chocolate dessert cups (optional)
Chocolate-Drizzled Fruit (see page 15 for directions) (optional)

POUR milk, orange juice and liqueur into small bowl. Add pudding mix. Beat with wire whisk until well blended, 1 to 2 minutes. Let stand 2 minutes or until slightly thickened. Fold in whipped topping. Spoon or pipe pudding mixture into chocolate cups or individual dessert glasses. Chill until set, about 1 hour. Garnish with Chocolate-Drizzled Fruit, if desired.
MAKES 4 to 6 servings

Prep time: 10 minutes
Chill time: 1 hour

Fruit in Cream

Vanilla Sauce (see Pear Fans, this page, for recipe)
Assorted fruit*
Quick Chocolate Sauce (recipe follows)
Mint leaves (optional)

SPOON Vanilla Sauce onto each serving plate to cover bottom. Swirl Quick Chocolate Sauce through Vanilla Sauce to form design (see page 12 for directions). Arrange fruit in sauce. Garnish with mint leaves, if desired.

*We suggest any variety of berries, mandarin orange sections, melon balls, halved seedless grapes, sliced peaches, kiwifruit or plums.

Quick Chocolate Sauce

¾ cup light corn syrup
1 package (4-serving size) JELL-O Instant Pudding and Pie Filling, Chocolate or Chocolate Fudge Flavor
¾ cup evaporated milk or half and half

POUR corn syrup into small bowl. Blend in pudding mix. Gradually add evaporated milk, stirring constantly. Let stand 10 minutes or until slightly thickened.

MAKES about 2 cups

Prep time: 20 minutes

Note: Store leftover sauces in covered container in refrigerator.

Pear Fans

Your guests will think you are an artist when they see these sauces.

Canned pear halves, drained
Vanilla Sauce (recipe follows)
Berry Cream Sauce (see page 26 for recipe)
Cinnamon stick, cut into ¾-inch pieces (optional)
Mint leaves (optional)

SLICE pears lengthwise, cutting almost through stem ends. Place on individual serving plates; spread to form fans (see page 11 for directions). Spoon Vanilla Sauce around pears. Swirl Berry Cream Sauce through Vanilla Sauce to form design (see page 12 for directions). Place cinnamon stick and mint leaf at stem end of each pear, if desired.

Vanilla Sauce

3½ cups cold half and half or milk
1 package (4-serving size) JELL-O Instant Pudding and Pie Filling, French Vanilla or Vanilla Flavor

POUR half and half into medium bowl. Add pudding mix. Beat with wire whisk until well blended, 1 to 2 minutes. Let stand 10 minutes or until slightly thickened.

MAKES 3½ cups

Prep time: 20 minutes

Top: Pear Fans; bottom:
Fruit in Cream

Berry Cream Sauce

2 packages (10 ounces each)
BIRDS EYE Quick Thaw Red
Raspberries or
Strawberries, thawed
1½ cups cold half and half or
milk
1 package (4-serving size)
JELL-O Instant Pudding
and Pie Filling, French
Vanilla or Vanilla Flavor

PLACE raspberries in food
processor or blender; cover.
Process until smooth; strain to
remove seeds. Pour half and half
into medium bowl. Add pudding
mix. Beat with wire whisk until
well blended, 1 to 2 minutes. Stir
in raspberry puree. Let stand 10
minutes or until slightly thickened.
Serve over cake or fruit.

MAKES 3½ cups

Note: Store leftover sauces in
covered containers in refrigerator.

Prep time: 5 minutes

Fruited Cream Brulee

½ pint raspberries*
1 cup cold milk
½ cup cold half and half
1 tablespoon orange liqueur or
orange juice
1 package (4-serving size)
JELL-O Instant Pudding
and Pie Filling, French
Vanilla or Vanilla Flavor
2 tablespoons light brown
sugar, sifted

COVER bottoms of 4 (6-ounce)
ovenproof dishes or custard cups
with raspberries.

POUR milk, half and half and
liqueur into small bowl. Add
pudding mix. Beat with wire whisk
until well blended, 1 to 2 minutes.
Let stand 2 minutes or until slightly
thickened. Pour over raspberries in
dishes. Chill 1 hour.

SPRINKLE pudding with brown
sugar. Broil until sugar melts and
bubbles. Garnish with additional
raspberries, if desired.

MAKES 4 servings

*1 cup sliced strawberries may be
substituted for raspberries.

Prep time: 15 minutes
Chill time: 1 hour

Creamy Macaroon Indulgence

Creamy Macaroon Indulgence

1½ cups cold milk
 1 cup (½ pint) sour cream
 2 tablespoons almond liqueur*
 1 package (4-serving size)
     JELL-O Instant Pudding
     and Pie Filling, any flavor
 ½ cup crumbled macaroon
     cookies

MIX together milk, sour cream and liqueur in small bowl until smooth. Add pudding mix. Beat with wire whisk until well blended, 1 to 2 minutes. Spoon ½ of the pudding mixture into individual dessert dishes.

SPRINKLE crumbled macaroons evenly over pudding. Top with remaining pudding. Chill until ready to serve. Garnish with additional cookies, if desired.

MAKES 4 servings

*¼ teaspoon almond extract may be substituted for the almond liqueur.

Prep time: 15 minutes

Orange Cream Timbales

Your guests will love the surprise inside these desserts.

1 package (4-serving size) JELL-O Brand Gelatin, Orange Flavor
1 cup boiling water
½ cup cold water
Ice cubes
1¾ cups (4 ounces) COOL WHIP Whipped Topping, thawed
1 can (11 ounces) mandarin orange sections, well drained
Mint leaves (optional)

DISSOLVE gelatin in boiling water. Combine cold water and ice cubes to make 1 cup. Add to gelatin, stirring until ice is melted. If necessary, place bowl in larger bowl of ice and water; let stand, stirring occasionally, until slightly thickened, about 5 minutes.

FOLD 1⅓ cups of the whipped topping into gelatin mixture. Pour ½ of the gelatin mixture evenly into 6 (6-ounce) custard cups, filling each cup about halfway. Place dollop of remaining whipped topping in center of each dessert; press orange section into each dollop. Fill cups with remaining gelatin mixture. Chill until firm, about 3 hours.

PLACE remaining orange sections in food processor or blender; cover. Process until smooth. Unmold gelatin cups onto individual dessert plates. Spoon orange puree around desserts. (Or, omit orange puree. Garnish desserts with whole orange sections and mint.) Garnish with mint leaves, if desired.

MAKES 4 servings

Prep time: 20 minutes
Chill time: 3 hours

Melon Bubbles

1 package (4-serving size) JELL-O Brand Gelatin, any flavor
¾ cup boiling water
½ cup cold water
Ice cubes
1 cup melon balls (cantaloupe, honeydew or watermelon)
Mint leaves (optional)

DISSOLVE gelatin in boiling water. Combine cold water and ice cubes to make 1¼ cups. Add to gelatin, stirring until slightly thickened. Remove any unmelted ice. Measure 1⅓ cups gelatin into small bowl; add melon. Pour into individual dessert glasses or serving bowl.

WHIP remaining gelatin at high speed of electric mixer until fluffy, thick and about doubled in volume. Spoon over gelatin in glasses. Chill until set, about 2 hours. Garnish with additional melon balls and mint leaves, if desired.

MAKES 6 to 8 (½-cup) servings

Prep time: 10 minutes
Chill time: 2 hours

Orange Cream Timbales

Napoleon Tarts

Only you will know how easy these tarts are to make. Your guests will think you spent hours on them.

1 package (17¼ ounces) frozen puff pastry sheets
1 cup cold milk
1 cup (½ pint) sour cream
1 package (4-serving size) JELL-O Instant Pudding and Pie Filling, any flavor
Quick Chocolate Sauce (see page 24 for recipe)

THAW pastry as directed on package. Preheat oven to 375°. Unfold pastry. Cut each sheet into 4 squares. Fold each square in half diagonally. (See Diagram 1.) Cut along 2 unfolded edges, leaving ½-inch rim all around (do not cut completely through to center). (See Diagram 2.) Unfold pastry. Fold outer top righthand corner (A) over to inner bottom lefthand corner (B); fold outer bottom lefthand corner (C) over to inner top righthand corner (D). (See Diagram 3.) Repeat with remaining squares.

PLACE pastries on baking sheets. Pierce bottom of each pastry in several places with fork. Bake for 12 to 15 minutes or until golden. If pastry rises in center, gently press down with fork. Cool on rack.

MIX milk and sour cream in small bowl until smooth. Add pudding mix. Beat with wire whisk until well blended, 1 to 2 minutes. Let stand 5 minutes or until slightly thickened.

SPOON 1 tablespoon Quick Chocolate Sauce onto bottom of each tart shell. Spoon pudding mixture into shells.

DRIZZLE each tart with 1 teaspoon Quick Chocolate Sauce in stripes. Pull wooden pick through stripes in an up and down motion to feather lines. Chill until ready to serve. Serve with remaining sauce.
MAKES 8 servings

Prep time: 20 minutes
Baking time: 12 minutes

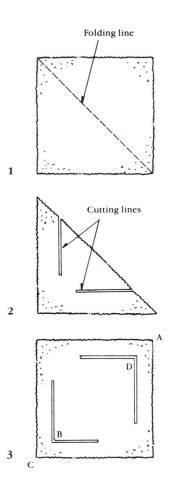

Napoleon Tarts

Tropical Breeze

1 package (4-serving size)
JELL-O Brand Gelatin, any
flavor
1½ cups boiling tropical blend
juice
1 tablespoon grated lemon,
orange or lime rind
½ cup cold water
Ice cubes
¾ cup light corn syrup
2 egg whites, lightly beaten

DISSOLVE gelatin in boiling juice;
stir in rind. Combine cold water
and ice cubes to make 1 cup. Add
to gelatin, stirring until ice is
melted. Stir in corn syrup and egg
whites. Place bowl in larger bowl
of ice and water. Let stand, stirring
occasionally, until gelatin is
slightly thickened, about 5
minutes.

BEAT gelatin mixture at high
speed of electric mixer until thick
and frothy. Pour into 9×5-inch loaf
pan. Freeze until firm, about 6
hours or overnight.

SCOOP frozen mixture into
individual dessert glasses. Garnish
with Citrus Curls (see page 9 for
directions), if desired.
MAKES 12 servings

NOTE: USE ONLY CLEAN EGGS
WITH NO CRACKS IN SHELL.

Prep time: 15 minutes
Freezing time: 6 hours

Pastry Chef Tarts

1 package (10 ounces) pie
crust mix
1 egg, beaten
1 to 2 tablespoons cold water
1½ cups cold half and half or
milk
1 package (4-serving size)
JELL-O Instant Pudding
and Pie Filling, French
Vanilla or Vanilla Flavor
Assorted berries or fruit*
Mint leaves (optional)

PREHEAT oven to 425°. Combine
pie crust mix with egg. Add just
enough water to form dough. Form
2 to 3 tablespoons dough into a
round. Press each round onto
bottom and sides of each 3- to 4-
inch tart pan. (Use tart pans with
removable bottoms, if possible.)
Pierce pastry several times with
fork. Place on baking sheet. Bake
for 10 minutes or until golden.
Cool slightly. Remove tart shells
from pans; cool completely on
racks.

POUR half and half into small
bowl. Add pudding mix. Beat with
wire whisk until well blended, 1 to
2 minutes. Spoon into tart shells.
Chill until ready to serve.

ARRANGE fruit on pudding.
Garnish with mint leaves, if
desired.   *MAKES 10 servings*

*We suggest any variety of berries,
mandarin orange sections, melon
balls, halved seedless grapes, sliced
peaches, kiwifruit or plums.

Note: Individual graham cracker
crumb tart shells may be
substituted for baked tart shells.

Prep time: 20 minutes
Baking time: 10 minutes

Pastry Chef Tarts

Holidays and More

Eggnog Cheesecake

You won't want to cut this dessert because it's so pretty, but please do. It tastes as good as it looks.

2 packages (5½ ounces each) chocolate-laced pirouette cookies
⅓ cup graham cracker crumbs
3 tablespoons PARKAY Margarine, melted
2 packages (8 ounces each) PHILADELPHIA BRAND Cream Cheese, softened
2 cups cold prepared eggnog
2 cups cold milk
2 packages (4-serving size each) JELL-O Instant Pudding and Pie Filling, French Vanilla or Vanilla Flavor
1 tablespoon rum
⅛ teaspoon ground nutmeg
COOL WHIP Whipped Topping, thawed (optional)
Ribbon (optional)

RESERVE 1 cookie for garnish, if desired. Cut 1-inch piece off 1 end of each of the remaining cookies. Crush 1-inch pieces into crumbs; set aside remaining cookies for sides of cake. Combine cookie crumbs, graham cracker crumbs and margarine until well mixed. Press mixture firmly onto bottom of 9-inch springform pan.

BEAT cream cheese at low speed of electric mixer until smooth. Gradually add 1 cup of the eggnog, blending until mixture is very smooth. Add remaining eggnog, milk, pudding mix, rum and nutmeg. Beat until well blended, about 1 minute. Pour cream cheese mixture carefully into pan. Chill until firm, about 3 hours. Run hot metal spatula or knife around edges of pan before removing sides.

PRESS remaining cookies, cut sides down, into sides of cake. Garnish with whipped topping and reserved cookie, if desired. Tie ribbon around cake, if desired.
MAKES 12 servings

Prep time: 45 minutes
Chill time: 3 hours

Top to bottom: Eggnog Cheesecake; Holiday Fruitcake (page 36); Marzipan Fruits (page 36); Raspberry Gift Box (page 37)

34

Holiday Fruitcake

A light cake with just a little bit of fruit. The Marzipan Fruits on top are easy to make and turn this dessert into a show stopper.

1 cup chopped candied fruit
⅔ cup pitted dates, chopped
½ cup chopped walnuts
¼ cup brandy or orange juice
1 package (6-serving size) JELL-O Instant Pudding and Pie Filling, Vanilla Flavor
1 package (2-layer size) yellow cake mix
4 eggs
1 cup (½ pint) sour cream
⅓ cup vegetable oil
1 tablespoon grated orange rind
⅔ cup cold milk
  Marzipan Fruits (recipe follows) (optional)

MIX together candied fruit, dates, walnuts and brandy.

RESERVE ⅓ cup pudding mix; set aside. Combine cake mix, remaining pudding mix, eggs, sour cream, oil and orange rind in large bowl. Beat at low speed of electric mixer just to moisten, scraping sides of bowl often. Beat at medium speed 4 minutes. Stir in fruit mixture.

POUR batter into well-greased and floured 10-inch fluted tube pan. Bake at 350° for 45 minutes or until cake tester inserted in center comes out clean. Cool in pan 15 minutes. Remove from pan; finish cooling on wire rack.

BEAT reserved pudding mix and milk in small bowl until smooth. Spoon over top of cake to glaze. Garnish with Marzipan Fruits, if desired.　　*MAKES 12 servings*

Prep time: 30 minutes
Baking time: 45 minutes

Marzipan Fruits

1¾ cups BAKER'S ANGEL FLAKE Coconut, finely chopped
1 package (4-serving size) JELL-O Brand Gelatin, any flavor
1 cup ground blanched almonds
⅔ cup sweetened condensed milk
1½ teaspoons sugar
1 teaspoon almond extract
  Food coloring (optional)
  Whole cloves (optional)
  Citron or angelica (optional)

MIX together coconut, gelatin, almonds, milk, sugar and extract. Shape by hand into small fruits, or use small candy molds. If desired, use food coloring to paint details on fruit; add whole cloves and citron for stems and blossom ends. Chill until dry. Store in covered container at room temperature up to 1 week.

MAKES 2 to 3 dozen confections

Prep time: 30 minutes

Raspberry Gift Box

This dessert is impressive as shown, but if you are pressed for time, omit the gumdrop ribbon and garnish with fresh raspberries.

2 packages (4-serving size each) or 1 package (8-serving size) JELL-O Brand Gelatin, Raspberry Flavor
1½ cups boiling water
¾ cup cran-raspberry juice
Ice cubes
3½ cups (8 ounces) COOL WHIP Whipped Topping, thawed
Raspberry Sauce (recipe follows)
Gumdrop Ribbon (see page 13 for directions) (optional)
Frosted Cranberries (see page 11 for directions) (optional)

DISSOLVE gelatin in boiling water. Combine cran-raspberry juice and ice cubes to make 1¾ cups. Add to gelatin, stirring until ice is melted. Chill until slightly thickened. Fold in whipped topping. Pour into 9×5-inch loaf pan. Chill until firm, about 4 hours.

PREPARE Raspberry Sauce, Gumdrop Ribbon and Frosted Cranberries, if desired.

UNMOLD gelatin mixture onto serving plate. Cut Gumdrop Ribbon into 2 (10×1-inch) strips and 1 (5×1-inch) strip. Place strips on raspberry loaf, piecing strips together as necessary, to resemble ribbon. Cut 7 (3×1-inch) strips; form into bow. Place on gumdrop ribbon. Decorate with Frosted Cranberries. Serve with Raspberry Sauce. *MAKES 8 servings*

Raspberry Sauce

2 packages (10 ounces each) BIRDS EYE Quick Thaw Red Raspberries, thawed
2 teaspoons cornstarch

PLACE raspberries in food processor or blender; cover. Process until smooth; strain to remove seeds. Combine cornstarch with small amount of the raspberries in medium saucepan; add remaining raspberries. Bring to boil over medium heat, stirring constantly; boil 1 minute. Chill.
MAKES 2 cups

Prep time: 30 minutes
Chill time: 4 hours

Christmas Tree Poke Cake

2 packages (2-layer size each) white cake mix
1 package (4-serving size) JELL-O Brand Gelatin, Strawberry Flavor
1 package (4-serving size) JELL-O Brand Gelatin, Lime Flavor
2 cups boiling water
2⅔ cups (7 ounces) BAKER'S ANGEL FLAKE Coconut
Green food coloring
5¼ cups (12 ounces) COOL WHIP Whipped Topping, thawed
Assorted gumdrops (optional)
Peppermint candies (optional)
Red string licorice (optional)

PREPARE 1 cake mix as directed on package. Pour batter into greased and floured 9-inch square pan. Bake at 325° for 50 to 55 minutes or until cake tester inserted in center comes out clean. Cool 10 minutes. Remove from pan; finish cooling on rack. Repeat with remaining cake mix.

PLACE cake layers, top sides up, in 2 clean 9-inch square pans. Pierce cakes with large fork at ½-inch intervals.

DISSOLVE each flavor of gelatin in separate bowl, using 1 cup of the boiling water for each. Carefully pour strawberry flavor gelatin over 1 cake layer and lime flavor gelatin over second cake layer. Chill 3 hours.

TOAST ⅓ cup of the coconut (see page 10 for directions); set aside. Tint remaining coconut with green food coloring (see page 10 for directions).

DIP 1 cake pan in warm water 10 seconds; unmold. Place right side up on large serving plate or cutting board. Cut cake as shown in Diagram 1. Arrange pieces in Christmas tree shape (Diagram 2), using small amount of whipped topping to hold pieces together. Top with about 1½ cups of the whipped topping. Unmold second cake layer; cut into pieces as shown in Diagram 1. Place pieces on first layer, using small amount of whipped topping to hold pieces together. Use remaining whipped topping to frost entire cake.

SPRINKLE trunk of tree with toasted coconut. Sprinkle remaining cake with green coconut. Decorate with gumdrops, peppermint candies and licorice, if desired. Chill until ready to serve.

MAKES 24 servings

Prep time: 30 minutes
Baking time: 50 minutes
Chill time: 3 hours

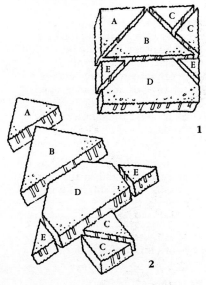

Christmas Popcorn Teddy Bear

"Teddy" is sure to become a Christmas classic, since he is as tasty as he is cute. You don't have to save him just for Christmas. Use this recipe to make all kinds of animals any time of year.

18 cups popped popcorn
1 cup light corn syrup
½ cup sugar
1 package (4-serving size) JELL-O Brand Gelatin, Strawberry or Lime Flavor
Jelly beans or gumdrops (optional)
Ribbon (optional)

PLACE popcorn in large greased bowl. Combine corn syrup and sugar in medium saucepan. Bring to full rolling boil, stirring constantly; boil 1 minute. Remove from heat. Stir in gelatin until dissolved. Pour over popcorn; toss to coat well. Cool 5 minutes.

FORM about ⅔ of the popcorn mixture into 2 balls, one larger than the other, forming bear's body and head. Shape remaining popcorn into arms, legs and ears; attach to body and head. Use jelly beans or gumdrops for eyes and nose. Attach ribbon bow tie, if desired.

MAKES 1 large teddy bear

Popcorn Balls: Prepare popcorn mixture as directed; shape into 2-inch balls. Makes about 2 dozen popcorn balls.

Note: For ease in handling, grease hands slightly before shaping popcorn mixture into desired shapes.

Prep time: 20 minutes

Ginger Bears

1½ cups all-purpose flour
1½ teaspoons ground ginger
1 teaspoon ground cinnamon
½ teaspoon baking soda
½ cup (1 stick) PARKAY Margarine
½ cup firmly packed brown sugar
1 package (4-serving size) JELL-O Pudding and Pie Filling, Butterscotch Flavor
1 egg
Confectioners Sugar Glaze (recipe follows) or 1 tube prepared decorating icing
Ribbon (optional)

MIX together flour, spices and baking soda. Beat margarine at low speed of electric mixer until light and fluffy; beat in sugar, pudding mix and egg. Gradually add flour mixture, beating until smooth after each addition. Chill dough until firm enough to handle.

ROLL out dough to ⅛-inch thickness on floured surface; cut with 3-inch floured teddy bear cookie cutter. Place on greased baking sheets. Bake at 350° for 10 minutes or until lightly browned. Remove; cool on rack. Decorate cooled cookies with Confectioners Sugar Glaze or icing. Attach ribbon bow ties, if desired.

MAKES about 2½ dozen cookies

Confectioners Sugar Glaze

2½ cups confectioners sugar
3 tablespoons (about) hot
   milk or water

PLACE sugar in small bowl.
Gradually add milk, blending well.
                    MAKES 1⅓ cups

Prep time: 30 minutes
Baking time: 30 minutes

*Top: Christmas Popcorn Teddy Bear
(page 40); bottom: Ginger Bears
(page 40)*

Eggnog Trifle

Make a day ahead, let the flavors blend, then relax and enjoy your New Year's Eve party.

1¼ cups cold milk
1 package (4-serving size) JELL-O Instant Pudding and Pie Filling, French Vanilla or Vanilla Flavor
¼ cup rum
⅛ teaspoon ground nutmeg
3½ cups (8 ounces) COOL WHIP Whipped Topping, thawed
1 pound cake loaf (about 12 ounces)
2 tablespoons strawberry jam
1 can (11 ounces) mandarin orange sections, drained
1½ cups strawberries, halved
¼ cup sliced almonds, toasted (see page 12 for directions)

POUR milk into medium bowl. Add pudding mix, 2 tablespoons of the rum and nutmeg. Beat with wire whisk until well blended, 1 to 2 minutes. Let stand 5 minutes or until slightly thickened. Fold in ½ of the whipped topping.

CUT rounded top off pound cake; reserve for snacking or other use. Slice remaining cake horizontally into 4 layers. Sprinkle layers evenly with remaining 2 tablespoons rum. Spread jam on surface of 2 layers; top with remaining 2 layers. Cut cakes into 1-inch cubes.

ARRANGE about ½ of the cake cubes on bottom of 2½-quart straight-sided bowl. Spoon ½ of the pudding mixture into bowl. Top with ½ of the fruit and almonds;

Clockwise from top left: Eggnog Trifle; Sparkling Champagne Dessert; Pink Champagne Sorbet (page 44)

cover with remaining cake cubes. Spoon remaining pudding mixture over cake. Top with remaining fruit and almonds. Garnish with remaining whipped topping. Chill until ready to serve.

MAKES 8 to 10 servings

Prep time: 30 minutes

Sparkling Champagne Dessert

Keep the champagne flowing, through dessert. This is a delicious way to top off a New Year's Eve dinner.

2 packages (4-serving size each) or 1 package (8-serving size) JELL-O Brand Gelatin, Lemon Flavor
2 cups boiling water
2 cups champagne or ginger ale
3 oranges, sectioned
Citrus Curls (see page 9 for directions) (optional)

DISSOLVE gelatin in boiling water. Let stand about 10 minutes to cool. Add champagne. Chill until slightly thickened.

MEASURE 1 cup gelatin into small bowl; set aside. Fold orange sections into remaining gelatin. Spoon into champagne glasses or dessert dishes.

BEAT reserved gelatin at high speed of electric mixer until fluffy, thick and about doubled in volume. Spoon over clear gelatin in glasses. Chill until firm, about 2 hours. Garnish with Citrus Curls, if desired. *MAKES 8 servings*

Prep time: 15 minutes
Chill time: 2 hours

Pink Champagne Sorbet

A light, refreshing way to end a special meal.

1 package (4-serving size)
  JELL-O Brand Gelatin,
  Strawberry Flavor
1⅓ cups boiling water
1 bottle (187 mL) pink
  champagne or ⅔ cup
  strawberry flavored soda
¾ cup light corn syrup
2 egg whites, lightly beaten
  Lime slices (optional)

DISSOLVE gelatin in boiling water.
Stir in champagne and corn syrup.
Beat in egg whites with wire whisk.
Pour into 13×9-inch pan. Freeze
until firm, about 2 hours.

SPOON ½ of the gelatin mixture
into food processor or blender;
cover. Process at high speed until
smooth but not melted, about 30
seconds. Pour into 9×5-inch loaf
pan. Repeat with remaining
mixture; pour over mixture in pan.
Cover; freeze until firm, about 6
hours or overnight.

SCOOP gelatin mixture into
dessert or champagne glasses.
Garnish with lime slices, if desired.
                MAKES 8 servings

NOTE: USE ONLY CLEAN EGGS
WITH NO CRACKS IN SHELL.

Prep time: 15 minutes
Freezing time: 8 hours

Elegant Raspberry Chocolate Pie

This pie is easy to make and guaranteed to impress that special someone.

1 package (4-serving size)
  JELL-O Brand Gelatin,
  Raspberry Flavor
1¼ cups boiling water
1 pint vanilla ice cream,
  softened
1 packaged chocolate crumb
  crust
3 tablespoons PARKAY
  Margarine
2 squares BAKER'S Semi-
  Sweet Chocolate
  COOL WHIP Whipped
  Topping, thawed
  (optional)
  Raspberries (optional)

DISSOLVE gelatin in boiling water.
Spoon in ice cream, stirring until
melted and smooth. Chill until
slightly thickened, about 10
minutes. Pour into crust. Chill
until firm, about 2 hours.

MELT margarine with chocolate;
cool. Spread over pie. Chill until
chocolate mixture hardens.
Garnish with whipped topping and
raspberries, if desired.
                MAKES 8 servings

Note: For ease in serving, let pie
stand 5 minutes after spreading on
chocolate. With knife, lightly score
pie into serving-size pieces. Chill
as directed above.

Prep time: 15 minutes
Chill time: 2½ hours

*Clockwise from top to bottom: Elegant
Raspberry Chocolate Pie; Fruit Terrine
Supreme (page 46); Raspberry
Bavarian (page 46)*

Fruit Terrine Supreme

2 packages (4-serving size each) or 1 package (8-serving size) JELL-O Brand Gelatin, Lemon Flavor
1½ cups boiling water
¾ cup orange juice
Ice cubes
2 teaspoons grated orange rind
3½ cups (8 ounces) COOL WHIP Whipped Topping, thawed
¼ cup sour cream
1 tablespoon milk
Strawberry Sauce (recipe follows)
Fruit (optional)

DISSOLVE gelatin in boiling water. Combine orange juice and ice cubes to make 1¾ cups. Add to gelatin, stirring until ice is melted. Stir in orange rind. Place bowl in larger bowl of ice and water. Let stand, stirring occasionally, until gelatin is slightly thickened, about 5 minutes.

FOLD whipped topping into gelatin mixture. Spoon into 8×4-inch loaf pan. Chill until firm, at least 3 hours. Unmold onto cutting board.

STIR together sour cream and milk. Spoon about 2 tablespoons of the Strawberry Sauce onto individual dessert plates. Swirl sour cream mixture through Strawberry Sauce to form design (see page 12 for directions). Slice terrine; place in sauce on plates. Garnish with fruit, if desired.

MAKES 8 to 10 servings

Strawberry Sauce

2 packages (10 ounces each) BIRDS EYE Quick Thaw Strawberries, thawed
2 teaspoons cornstarch

PLACE strawberries in food processor or blender; cover. Process until smooth. Combine cornstarch with small amount of the strawberries in medium saucepan; add remaining strawberries. Bring to boil over medium heat, stirring constantly; boil 1 minute. Chill.

MAKES 2 cups

Prep time: 30 minutes
Chill time: 3 hours

✓ Raspberry Bavarian

Don't tell your Valentine how easy this souffle is to make.

1 package (4-serving size) JELL-O Brand Gelatin, Raspberry Flavor
¾ cup boiling water
½ cup cold water
Ice cubes
1¾ cups (4 ounces) COOL WHIP Whipped Topping, thawed
Raspberries (optional)
Mint leaves (optional)

DISSOLVE gelatin in boiling water. Combine cold water and ice cubes to make 1 cup. Add to gelatin, stirring until ice is melted. Place bowl in larger bowl of ice and water. Let stand, stirring occasionally, until gelatin is slightly thickened, about 5 minutes. Fold in whipped topping.

SPOON gelatin mixture into individual souffle cups with paper collars (see note below). Chill until firm, about 2 hours. Remove collars. Garnish with raspberries and mint leaves, if desired.

MAKES 4 servings

Note: To make collars, cut pieces of waxed paper or foil long enough to wrap around dishes and overlap slightly; fold in half lengthwise. Wrap doubled paper around dish, extending about 1 inch above rim. Secure with tape.

Prep time: 20 minutes
Chill time: 2 hours

Truffle Treats

6 squares BAKER'S Semi-Sweet Chocolate
¼ cup (½ stick) PARKAY Margarine
2⅔ cups (7 ounces) BAKER'S ANGEL FLAKE Coconut
1 package (8 ounces) PHILADELPHIA BRAND Cream Cheese, softened
2½ cups cold half and half or milk
1 package (6-serving size) JELL-O Instant Pudding and Pie Filling, Chocolate Flavor
2 tablespoons unsweetened cocoa
1 tablespoon confectioners sugar

PLACE chocolate in heavy saucepan over very low heat; stir constantly until just melted. Remove 2 tablespoons of the melted chocolate; set aside.

STIR margarine into remaining chocolate in saucepan until melted. Gradually stir in coconut, tossing to coat evenly. Press mixture into 13×9-inch pan which has been lined with foil.

BEAT cream cheese at medium speed of electric mixer until smooth; beat in reserved 2 tablespoons chocolate. Gradually mix in half and half. Add pudding mix. Beat at low speed until well blended, about 1 minute. Pour over crust. Freeze until firm, about 4 hours or overnight.

MIX together cocoa and sugar in small bowl; sift over truffle mixture. Lift from pan onto cutting board; let stand 10 minutes to soften slightly. Cut into diamonds, squares or triangles.

MAKES about 20 pieces

Prep time: 15 minutes
Freezing time: 4 hours

Easter Bonnet Cake

It's almost too pretty to eat.

1 package (2-layer size)
   yellow cake mix
2 packages (4-serving size
   each) JELL-O Instant
   Pudding and Pie Filling,
   Lemon Flavor
4 eggs
1 cup water
¼ cup vegetable oil
1½ cups cold milk
3½ cups (8 ounces) COOL WHIP
   Whipped Topping, thawed
2⅔ cups (7 ounces) BAKER'S
   ANGEL FLAKE Coconut
   Cloth ribbon (optional)
   Gumdrop Flowers (see page
   13 for directions)
   (optional)

COMBINE cake mix, 1 package of
the pudding mix, eggs, water and
oil in large bowl. Beat at low speed
of electric mixer just to moisten,
scraping sides of bowl often. Beat
at medium speed 4 minutes. Pour
3¼ cups of the batter into greased
and floured 1½-quart metal or
ovenproof glass bowl; pour
remaining batter into greased and
floured 12-inch pizza pan. Bake at
350° for 15 minutes for the pan
and 50 minutes for the bowl or
until cake tester inserted in centers
comes out clean.

COOL cakes 10 minutes. Remove
from pan and bowl; finish cooling
on racks. If necessary, cut thin slice
from flat end of bowl-shaped cake
so that it will sit flat; split
horizontally into 3 layers.

POUR milk into small bowl. Add
remaining package of pudding mix.
Beat with wire whisk until well
blended, 1 to 2 minutes.

PLACE 12-inch cake layer on large
serving plate or tray. Spread layer
with 1½ cups of the whipped
topping. Center bottom layer of
bowl-shaped cake on frosted layer;
spread with ⅔ of the pudding. Add
second layer; spread with
remaining pudding. Add top layer,
forming the crown.

SPREAD remaining whipped
topping over crown. Sprinkle
coconut over cake. Tie ribbon
around cake crown to form hat
band and bow and garnish with
Gumdrop Flowers, if desired. Chill
until ready to serve.

MAKES 16 servings

Prep time: 45 minutes
Baking time: 50 minutes

Gelatin Easter Baskets

*Why use wicker baskets when you
can make these baskets and eat
them, too?*

1 package (4-serving size)
   JELL-O Brand Gelatin,
   any flavor
1 cup boiling water
½ cup cold water
½ cup BAKER'S ANGEL FLAKE
   Coconut
   Food coloring
   Jelly beans
   Red string licorice

DISSOLVE gelatin in boiling water.
Add cold water. Pour into
individual ring molds or 6-ounce
custard cups. Chill until firm,
about 2 hours.

TINT coconut as desired with food
coloring (see page 10 for
directions).

UNMOLD gelatin onto individual dessert plates. Sprinkle coconut into center of each mold for "grass." Place jelly beans on top of coconut. Cut licorice for basket handles; insert in molds.

MAKES 4 servings

Prep time: 15 minutes
Chill time: 2 hours

Top: Easter Bonnet Cake (page 48); bottom: Gelatin Easter Baskets (page 48)

Top: Stars and Stripes (page 51);
bottom: Lemon Strawberry Stars

Lemon Strawberry Stars

1 pound cake loaf (about
   12 ounces)
1 package (4-serving size)
   JELL-O Instant Pudding
   and Pie Filling, Lemon
   Flavor
2 cups cold milk
   Sliced strawberries
   Strawberry Sauce (see page
   46 for recipe) (optional)

SLICE pound cake horizontally
into 5 layers. Cut each layer into 2
star shapes with large cookie
cutter. (Reserve cake scraps for
snacking or other use.)

PREPARE pudding mix with milk
as directed on package.

TOP ½ of the pound cake stars
with ½ of the sliced strawberries
and ½ of the pudding. Cover with
remaining stars, strawberries and
pudding. Serve with Strawberry
Sauce, if desired.

MAKES 5 servings

Prep time: 15 minutes

Stars and Stripes

Buy frozen puff pastry from your supermarket and you are home free! The results will create fireworks.

1 sheet frozen puff pastry dough
1 egg, lightly beaten
1½ cups cold half and half or milk
1 package (4-serving size) JELL-O Instant Pudding and Pie Filling, French Vanilla or Vanilla Flavor
Blueberries
Raspberries
COOL WHIP Whipped Topping, thawed

THAW puff pastry as directed on package. Unfold pastry to 10×9-inch rectangle. Cut 4 (½-inch) strips from 1 (9-inch) side of rectangle as shown in Diagram 1. (Remaining rectangle will measure 9×8 inches.) Cut 1 inch off each of 2 strips to make 2 (8-inch) strips (Diagram 2); discard 1-inch pieces. (You should have 2 8-inch strips and 2 9-inch strips.)

PLACE pastry on baking sheet. Brush with egg. Place strips on top of each side of rectangle to form rim; lightly press strips to base. Brush strips with egg. Pierce bottom of pastry in several places with fork. Chill 20 minutes. Meanwhile, preheat oven to 425°. Bake pastry for 12 to 15 minutes or until golden. (If center of pastry rises, gently press down with fork.) Cool on rack.

POUR half and half into small bowl. Add pudding mix. Beat with wire whisk until well blended, 1 to 2 minutes. Spoon pudding into pastry shell. Chill until set, about 1 hour.

ARRANGE fruit on top of pudding in alternating stripes of blueberries and raspberries. Pipe "stars" of whipped topping around borders.
MAKES 8 to 10 servings

Prep time: 20 minutes
Chill time: 1 hour

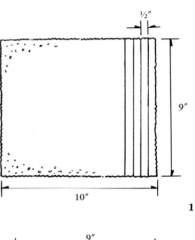

1

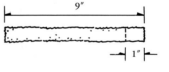

2

Spiced Cranberry-Orange Mold

1 bag (12 ounces) cranberries*
½ cup sugar*
2 packages (4-serving size
   each) or 1 package
   (8-serving size) JELL-O
   Brand Gelatin, Orange or
   Lemon Flavor
1½ cups boiling water
1 cup cold water*
1 tablespoon lemon juice
¼ teaspoon ground cinnamon
⅛ teaspoon ground cloves
1 orange, sectioned and diced
½ cup chopped walnuts
   Orange slices (optional)
   White kale or curly leaf
   lettuce (optional)

PLACE cranberries in food
processor; cover. Process until
finely chopped. Mix with sugar; set
aside.

DISSOLVE gelatin in boiling water.
Add cold water, lemon juice and
spices. Chill until thickened. Fold
in cranberry mixture, oranges and
walnuts. Spoon into 5-cup mold.
Chill until firm, about 4 hours.
Unmold. Garnish with orange
slices and kale, if desired.
                    MAKES 10 servings

*1 can (16 ounces) whole berry
cranberry sauce may be substituted
for fresh cranberries. Omit sugar
and reduce cold water to ½ cup.

Prep time: 20 minutes
Chill time: 4 hours

Harvest Pie

1 cup cold milk
1 package (4-serving size)
   JELL-O Instant Pudding
   and Pie Filling, French
   Vanilla or Vanilla Flavor
2 cups thawed COOL WHIP
   Whipped Topping
1 packaged graham cracker
   crumb crust
1 apple, chopped
½ cup chopped pecans or
   walnuts
¼ cup KRAFT Miniature
   Marshmallows
¼ cup caramel sauce or ice
   cream topping

POUR milk into medium bowl.
Add pie filling mix. Beat with wire
whisk until well blended, 1 to 2
minutes. Let stand 1 to 2 minutes
or until slightly thickened.

FOLD whipped topping into filling
mixture. Pour into crust. Chill
until firm, about 2 hours. Sprinkle
with apples, pecans and
marshmallows just before serving.
Drizzle caramel sauce over pie.
                    MAKES 8 servings

Prep time: 15 minutes
Chill time: 2 hours

Maple Walnut Cheesecake

⅓ cup PARKAY Margarine
⅓ cup finely chopped walnuts
1 package (11 ounces) JELL-O
   No Bake Cheesecake mix
1½ cups cold milk
2 tablespoons maple flavor
   syrup
¼ teaspoon ground cinnamon
¾ cup walnut topping

Top: Harvest Pie (page 52); bottom:
Maple Walnut Cheesecake (page 52)

MELT margarine in small skillet. Add walnuts; cook until lightly toasted, about 3 minutes. Stir in cheesecake crust crumbs. Press crumb mixture onto bottom of 8-inch square pan which has been lined with foil.

MIX milk with cheesecake filling mix, syrup and cinnamon at low speed of electric mixer until well blended. Beat at medium speed 3 minutes. Spread over crust. Chill until firm, at least 1 hour.

HEAT topping just before serving. Cut cheesecake into squares. Serve with warmed topping.
MAKES 8 servings

Prep time: 15 minutes
Chill time: 1 hour

Pumpkin Flan

1 package (4½ ounces) JELL-O
   AMERICANA Custard Mix*
2½ cups milk
2 teaspoons grated orange
   rind
¼ teaspoon ground cinnamon
1 egg yolk
1 cup canned pumpkin
   Citrus Fan (see page 10 for
   directions) (optional)
   Mint leaves (optional)

COMBINE custard mix, milk,
orange rind and cinnamon in
medium saucepan; mix in egg yolk.
Cook, stirring constantly, over
medium-low heat until mixture
comes to full boil. Remove from
heat. Add pumpkin, stirring until
well mixed. Pour into 1½-quart
souffle dish or bowl. Chill until
firm, about 3 hours.

DIP flan in hot water; unmold onto
serving plate. Garnish with Citrus
Fan and mint leaves, if desired.
                    MAKES 8 servings

*1 package (4-serving size) JELL-O
Pudding and Pie Filling, Vanilla
Flavor, may be substituted for the
custard mix.

Prep time: 15 minutes
Chill time: 3 hours

*New variations on an old
theme. They're wonderful!*

Thanksgiving Cranberry Pie

1 package (15 ounces)
   refrigerated pie crust
   (2 crusts)
1 package (4-serving size)
   JELL-O Brand Gelatin,
   Orange Flavor or any red
   flavor
¾ cup boiling water
½ cup orange juice
1 can (8 ounces) jellied or
   whole berry cranberry
   sauce
1 teaspoon grated orange rind
1 cup cold half and half or
   milk
1 package (4-serving size)
   JELL-O Instant Pudding
   and Pie Filling, French
   Vanilla or Vanilla Flavor
1 cup thawed COOL WHIP
   Whipped Topping
   Frosted Cranberries (see
   page 11 for directions)
   (optional)

PREPARE and bake 1 sheet of the
pie crust in 9-inch pie plate as
directed on package; cool. Cut out
leaf shapes from remaining sheet of
pie crust with small cookie cutter.
Place on ungreased baking sheet;
bake at 450° for 8 minutes or until
golden. Cool.

DISSOLVE gelatin in boiling water.
Add orange juice. Place bowl in
larger bowl of ice and water. Let
stand, stirring occasionally, until
gelatin is slightly thickened, about
5 minutes. Stir in cranberry sauce
and orange rind. Spoon into pie
crust. Chill just until set, about
30 minutes.

Top: Pumpkin Flan (page 54); bottom: Thanksgiving Cranberry Pie (page 54)

POUR half and half into medium bowl. Add pie filling mix. Beat with wire whisk until well blended, 1 to 2 minutes. Let stand 2 minutes or until slightly thickened. Fold in whipped topping. Gently spread over gelatin mixture. Place pastry leaves around rim of pie. Chill until firm, about 2 hours. Garnish with additional whipped topping and Frosted Cranberries, if desired.

MAKES 8 servings

Prep time: 30 minutes
Baking time: 20 minutes
Chill time: 2½ hours

Festive Celebrations

Lemon Cheese Tart

2 packages (11 ounces each)
    JELL-O No-Bake
    Cheesecake mix
¼ cup sugar
⅔ cup PARKAY Margarine,
    melted
2 packages (4-serving size
    each) or 1 package
    (8-serving size) JELL-O
    Brand Gelatin, Lemon
    Flavor
2 cups boiling water
1 cup cold water
3 cups cold milk
1½ teaspoons grated lemon rind
    (optional)
1 cup (about) seedless red or
    green grapes, halved
    Mint leaves

MIX cheesecake crust crumbs with sugar in 9-inch springform pan. Stir in margarine. Press crumb mixture firmly onto bottom of pan.

DISSOLVE gelatin in boiling water. Add cold water. Chill until slightly thickened.

MIX milk with cheesecake filling mix and lemon rind at low speed of electric mixer until blended. Beat at medium speed 3 minutes. Pour over crust. Arrange grape halves on top of cheesecake to resemble large grape cluster. Place mint leaves at stem end of cluster. Carefully spoon thickened gelatin over grape cluster and filling. Chill until set, about 3 hours. Run hot metal spatula or knife around edge of pan before removing sides of pan.   *MAKES 12 servings*

Note: This recipe may be prepared 1 day ahead.

Prep time: 30 minutes
Chill time: 3 hours

Clockwise from top left: Lemon Cheese Tart; Sparkling Punch Bowl (page 58); Almond Heart Napoleons (page 58)

Sparkling Punch Bowl

Prepare this dessert 1 day ahead.

8 packages (4-serving size each) or 4 packages (8-serving size each) JELL-O Brand Gelatin, any flavor
8 cups boiling water
1 bottle (1 liter) ginger ale
Ice cubes
5 cups cut-up fruit*
1 can (20 ounces) pineapple chunks in juice, drained
Mint leaves (optional)

DISSOLVE gelatin in boiling water. Combine ginger ale and ice cubes to make 8 cups. Add to gelatin, stirring until slightly thickened. Remove any unmelted ice. Measure 4 cups of the gelatin; set aside. Fold cut-up fruit and pineapple chunks into remaining gelatin. Pour into large punch bowl. Chill until set but not firm.

WHIP reserved gelatin at high speed of electric mixer until fluffy, thick and about doubled in volume. Spoon over gelatin in punch bowl. Chill until firm, about 2 hours. Garnish with additional fruit and mint leaves, if desired.

MAKES 32 servings

*We suggest sliced bananas, strawberries or grapes.

Note: If large punch bowl is not available, use smaller bowl and pour extra gelatin mixture into punch cups.

Prep time: 20 minutes
Chill time: 2 hours

Almond Heart Napoleons

1 package (17¼ ounces) frozen puff pastry sheets
1¼ cups cold half and half or milk
2 tablespoons almond liqueur*
1 package (4-serving size) JELL-O Instant Pudding and Pie Filling, French Vanilla or Vanilla Flavor
½ cup confectioners sugar
2 teaspoons (about) hot water
1 square BAKER'S Semi-Sweet Chocolate, melted

THAW puff pastry as directed on package. Preheat oven to 350°. Unfold pastry. Using 2-inch heart-shaped cookie cutter, cut each sheet into 12 hearts. Bake on ungreased baking sheets for 20 minutes or until golden. Remove from baking sheets. Cool on racks. When pastry is completely cooled, split each heart horizontally in half.

POUR half and half and liqueur into small bowl. Add pudding mix. Beat with wire whisk until well blended, 1 to 2 minutes. Chill 10 minutes.

SPREAD about 1 tablespoon of the pudding mixture onto bottom half of each pastry; top with remaining pastry half.

STIR together confectioners sugar and hot water in small bowl to make thin glaze. Spread over hearts. (If glaze becomes too thick, add more hot water until glaze is of desired consistency.) Before glaze dries, drizzle chocolate on top to form thin lines. Draw wooden pick through chocolate to make design. Chill until ready to serve.

MAKES 2 dozen pastries

*½ teaspoon almond extract may be substituted for 2 tablespoons almond liqueur.

Note: Pastry may be cut and baked 1 day ahead. Assemble recipe no more than 6 hours before serving.

Prep time: 30 minutes
Baking time: 20 minutes

Pineapple Bombe

2 cans (20 ounces each) pineapple slices, drained
8 maraschino cherries, stemmed and halved
2½ cups cold milk
2 packages (4-serving size each) JELL-O Instant Pudding and Pie Filling, French Vanilla or Vanilla Flavor
3½ cups (8 ounces) COOL WHIP Whipped Topping, thawed
1 pound cake loaf (about 12 ounces), cut into 14 slices

LINE 2-quart bowl with plastic wrap. Arrange about 16 pineapple slices on bottom and sides of lined bowl, pushing slices as closely together as possible. Place cherry half, cut side up, in center of each pineapple slice.

POUR milk into large bowl. Add pudding mix. Beat with wire whisk until well blended, 1 to 2 minutes. Let stand 5 minutes. Fold in ½ of the whipped topping.

SPREAD about ⅓ of the pudding mixture over pineapple in bowl. Place about 6 cake slices over pudding layer; press down gently. Arrange 5 pineapple slices over cake slices. Layer with ⅓ of the pudding mixture, 4 cake slices and remaining pineapple. Cover with remaining pudding; top with remaining cake slices. Press down gently. Cover with plastic wrap. Chill at least 1 hour.

INVERT dessert onto serving platter. Carefully remove plastic wrap. Garnish with remaining whipped topping.

MAKES 16 servings

Prep time: 30 minutes
Chill time: 1 hour

Fruity Cheese Spread

2 packages (8 ounces each)
PHILADELPHIA BRAND
Cream Cheese, softened
1 package (4-serving size)
JELL-O Brand Gelatin,
any flavor
¼ cup chopped pecans
Assorted fresh fruit, cookies
and crackers*

BEAT cream cheese in large bowl
until smooth. Beat in gelatin until
well blended. Form mixture into
5-inch round. Cover with plastic
wrap. Chill about 1 hour.

REMOVE plastic wrap. Press
pecans gently around edges of
cheese round. Serve with fruit,
cookies and crackers.

MAKES 2 cups

*We suggest sliced apples or pears,
grapes and strawberries.

Note: Cheese round may be made 2
days ahead and refrigerated; let
stand at room temperature 15
minutes before serving.

Prep time: 15 minutes
Chill time: 1 hour

Fruit-Topped Lemon Cheese Squares

15 whole graham crackers,
broken in half
2 packages (8 ounces each)
PHILADELPHIA BRAND
Cream Cheese, softened
3 cups cold milk
2 packages (6-serving size
each) JELL-O Instant
Pudding and Pie Filling,
Lemon Flavor
1¾ cups (4 ounces) COOL WHIP
Whipped Topping, thawed
1 can (21 ounces) pie filling,
any fruit flavor

ARRANGE ½ of the crackers on
bottom of 13×9-inch pan, cutting
crackers to fit, if necessary.

BEAT cream cheese at low speed of
electric mixer until smooth.
Gradually beat in 1 cup of the
milk. Add pudding mix and
remaining milk. Beat at low speed
until well blended, 1 to 2 minutes.
Fold in whipped topping.

SPREAD ½ of the pudding mixture
over crackers. Add second layer of
crackers; top with remaining
pudding mixture. Freeze 2 hours.
Let stand at room temperature 15
minutes before cutting into
squares. Spoon pie filling over
each square.

MAKES 18 servings

Prep time: 20 minutes
Freezing time: 2 hours

*Clockwise from top left: Fruit-Topped
Lemon Cheese Squares; Pineapple
Bombe (page 59); Fruity Cheese
Spread*

Lemon Berry Terrine

1 pound cake loaf (about
    12 ounces)
1 package (8 ounces)
    PHILADELPHIA BRAND
    Cream Cheese, softened
2 cups cold milk
1 package (4-serving size)
    JELL-O Instant Pudding
    and Pie Filling, Lemon
    Flavor
1 teaspoon grated lemon rind
3½ cups (8 ounces) COOL WHIP
    Whipped Topping, thawed
1 pint strawberries, stems
    removed

LINE bottom and sides of 8×4-inch loaf pan with waxed paper.

CUT rounded top off pound cake; reserve for snacking or other use. Trim crusts from pound cake. Cut cake horizontally into 5 slices. Line bottom and long sides of loaf pan with 3 cake slices. Cut another cake slice in half; place on short sides of pan.

BEAT cream cheese at medium speed of electric mixer until smooth. Gradually beat in 1 cup of the milk. Add pudding mix, remaining 1 cup milk and lemon rind. Beat at low speed until blended, 1 to 2 minutes. Fold in 1½ cups of the whipped topping.

SPOON ½ of the filling into loaf pan. Reserve several strawberries for garnish. Arrange remaining strawberries in filling, pressing down slightly. Top with remaining filling. Place remaining cake slice on top of filling. Chill until firm, about 3 hours.

UNMOLD dessert onto serving plate; remove waxed paper. Garnish with remaining whipped topping and strawberries.

        MAKES 16 servings

Prep time: 30 minutes
Chill time: 3 hours

Apricot Pear Tart

1⅓ cups shortbread cookie or
    graham cracker crumbs
2 tablespoons sugar
¼ cup PARKAY Margarine,
    melted
1 package (4-serving size)
    JELL-O Brand Gelatin,
    Apricot Flavor
1 cup boiling water
⅔ cup cold water
1¾ cups (4 ounces) COOL WHIP
    Whipped Topping, thawed
½ teaspoon ground ginger
1 can (16 ounces) pear halves,
    drained
    Mint leaves
    Cinnamon stick, cut into
    ¾-inch pieces

MIX together cookie crumbs, sugar and margarine in small bowl. Press crumb mixture onto bottom of 9-inch springform pan.

DISSOLVE gelatin in boiling water. Add cold water. Measure ¾ cup gelatin; set aside. Chill remaining gelatin until slightly thickened. Fold in whipped topping and ginger. Spoon over crust.

CHILL measured gelatin until slightly thickened. Slice pears lengthwise, cutting almost through stem ends; arrange on whipped topping mixture in pan, fanning each pear slightly (see page 11 for

directions). Place mint leaf and cinnamon stick at stem end of each pear. Carefully spoon thickened gelatin over pears and filling. Chill until firm, about 3 hours. Run hot metal spatula or knife around edge of pan before removing sides of pan.   *MAKES 12 servings*

Prep time: 30 minutes
Chill time: 3 hours

Clockwise from top: Apricot Pear Tart (page 62); JELL-O Creamy Jigglers (page 83); Lemon Berry Terrine (page 62)

63

Mitt Cut-Up Cake

1 package (2-layer size) yellow
   cake mix
1 cup cold milk
1 package (4-serving size)
   JELL-O Instant Pudding
   and Pie Filling, Chocolate
   or Chocolate Fudge Flavor
3½ cups (8 ounces) COOL WHIP
   Whipped Topping, thawed
   Chocolate sprinkles
   String licorice
   JELL-O Jigglers (see page 83
   for recipe) (optional)

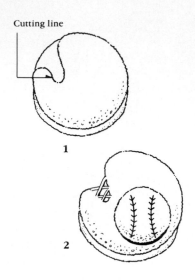

Cutting line

1

2

PREPARE cake mix as directed on package. Pour 2 cups of the batter into greased and floured 1-quart ovenproof bowl; pour remaining batter into greased and floured 9-inch round cake pan. Bake at 325° for 50 minutes or until cake tester inserted in centers comes out clean. Cool 15 minutes. Remove from pan and bowl; finish cooling on racks. Cut cake as shown in Diagram 1.

POUR milk into medium bowl. Add pudding mix. Beat with wire whisk until well blended, 1 to 2 minutes. Fold in 2½ cups of the whipped topping.

SPREAD pudding mixture over sides and top of 9-inch layer. Use remaining whipped topping to cover bowl-shaped cake; place over 9-inch layer. Decorate with chocolate sprinkles and licorice to resemble mitt and ball (Diagram 2). Chill cake until ready to serve. Arrange star-shaped Jigglers around cake, if desired.

MAKES 12 servings

Prep time: 30 minutes
Baking time: 50 minutes

Snack Mix

4 cups popped popcorn
2 cups thin pretzel sticks
2 cups crisp corn cereal
   squares
1 cup peanuts
½ cup raisins
6 tablespoons PARKAY
   Margarine, melted
1 package (4-serving size)
   JELL-O Brand Gelatin, any
   flavor

PLACE popcorn, pretzels, cereal, peanuts and raisins in large bowl. Add margarine; toss to coat well. Sprinkle with gelatin; toss until evenly coated.

MAKES 10 cups

Prep time: 10 minutes

*Clockwise from top left: Winner's
Circle Layered Dessert (page 66);
Snack Mix; Mitt Cut-Up Cake; JELL-O
Jigglers (page 83)*

Winner's Circle Layered Dessert

4½ cups cold milk
  3 packages (4-serving size each) JELL-O Instant Pudding and Pie Filling, French Vanilla or Vanilla Flavor
1¾ cups (4 ounces) COOL WHIP Whipped Topping, thawed
  4 packages (4-serving size each) or 2 packages (8-serving size each) JELL-O Brand Gelatin, Strawberry Flavor
  3 cups boiling water
  2 cups cold water
    Ice cubes
  2 cups blueberries
  2 cups sliced strawberries

POUR milk into large bowl. Add pudding mix. Beat with wire whisk until well blended, 1 to 2 minutes. Let stand 5 minutes. Fold in 1 cup of the whipped topping; chill.

DISSOLVE ½ of the gelatin in 1½ cups of the boiling water. Combine 1 cup of the cold water and ice cubes to make 1½ cups. Add to dissolved gelatin, stirring until slightly thickened. Remove any unmelted ice. Stir in ½ of the blueberries and strawberries. Spoon into 4-quart bowl. Chill 15 minutes or until thickened. Meanwhile, prepare remaining gelatin as directed above. Stir in remaining fruit.

TOP gelatin mixture in serving bowl with ½ of the pudding mixture, then remaining gelatin mixture. Chill 15 minutes or until thickened. Top with remaining pudding mixture. Chill until firm, about 3 hours. Garnish with remaining whipped topping and additional fruit, if desired.

MAKES 32 servings

Prep time: 30 minutes
Chill time: 4 hours

Chocolate Berry Torte

"Berry" beautiful and delicious.

  1 package (2-layer size) chocolate cake mix
  1 package (4-serving size) JELL-O Instant Pudding and Pie Filling, Chocolate or Chocolate Fudge Flavor
  4 eggs
  1 cup water
  ¼ cup vegetable oil
  3 cups cold milk
  2 tablespoons chocolate or coffee liqueur (optional)
  2 packages (4-serving size each) JELL-O Instant Pudding and Pie Filling, French Vanilla or Vanilla Flavor
1¾ cups (4 ounces) COOL WHIP Whipped Topping, thawed
  2 pints strawberries

COMBINE cake mix, chocolate pudding mix, eggs, water and oil in large bowl. Blend at low speed of electric mixer just to moisten, scraping sides of bowl often. Beat at medium speed 4 minutes. Pour into 2 greased and floured 9-inch round cake pans. Bake at 350° for 35 to 40 minutes or until cake tester inserted in centers comes out clean. Cool in pans 15 minutes. Remove from pans; finish cooling on racks.

POUR milk and liqueur into large bowl. Add vanilla pudding mix. Beat with wire whisk until well blended, 1 to 2 minutes. Let stand 5 minutes. Fold in whipped topping. Chill 15 minutes.

CUT each cake layer in half horizontally. Reserve a few strawberries for garnish; slice remaining strawberries. Place 1 cake layer on serving plate; top with ¼ of the pudding mixture and ⅓ of the sliced strawberries. Repeat layers, using remaining cake, pudding mixture and sliced strawberries, ending with pudding mixture. Chill at least 1 hour. Garnish with reserved strawberries.

MAKES 12 servings

Prep time: 30 minutes
Baking time: 35 minutes
Chill time: 1 hour

Butterfly Cupcakes

1 cup cold milk
1 package (4-serving size) JELL-O Instant Pudding and Pie Filling, any flavor
3½ cups (8 ounces) COOL WHIP Whipped Topping, thawed
24 cupcakes
Sprinkles
Pastel confetti candies
Black string licorice, cut into 2-inch strips

POUR milk into medium bowl. Add pudding mix. Beat with wire whisk until well blended, 1 to 2 minutes. Fold in whipped topping. Reserve 1 teaspoon pudding mixture.

CUT tops off cupcakes. Cut each top in half; set aside. Spoon 2 heaping tablespoons pudding mixture onto each cupcake; top with sprinkles. For each cupcake, insert 2 top halves of cupcake, cut sides together, in pudding mixture, raising outside ends slightly to resemble butterfly wings. Lightly dip confetti candies into reserved pudding mixture; arrange on cupcake wings. Insert string licorice in pudding mixture to resemble antennae. Chill until ready to serve.

MAKES 2 dozen cupcakes

Prep time: 25 minutes

Happy Birthday Dessert

A nice alternative or addition to birthday cake.

    1 package (4-serving size)
      JELL-O Brand Gelatin, any
      flavor except lemon
    5 cups boiling water
    2¼ cups cold water
    4 packages (4-serving size
      each) or 2 packages
      (8-serving size each)
      JELL-O Brand Gelatin,
      Lemon Flavor
    1 pint vanilla ice cream,
      softened
      COOL WHIP Whipped
      Topping, thawed
      (optional)

DISSOLVE 1 package gelatin (not lemon) in 1 cup of the boiling water. Add ¼ cup of the cold water. Pour into 9-inch square pan. Chill until firm.

DISSOLVE lemon gelatin in remaining 4 cups boiling water. Remove 2 cups gelatin and mix with remaining 2 cups cold water; chill until slightly thickened. Spoon ice cream into remaining gelatin, stirring until melted and smooth. Pour into 13×9-inch baking dish or pan. Chill until set but not firm. Top with clear lemon gelatin. Chill until set, about 3 hours.

CUT gelatin in 9-inch pan with alphabet cookie cutters to spell "Happy Birthday." (Cut remaining gelatin into cubes; reserve for snacking or other use.) Carefully transfer cutouts to top of gelatin. Garnish with whipped topping, if desired.   *MAKES 18 servings*

Prep time: 30 minutes
Chill time: 3 hours

Pineapple Party Cake

Try this refreshing fruit topping as an alternative to buttercream frosting.

    1 package (4-serving size)
      JELL-O Brand Gelatin,
      Orange Flavor
    ¾ cup boiling water
    1 can (8 ounces) crushed
      pineapple in juice,
      undrained
    1½ cups ice cubes
    2 baked 9-inch yellow or
      white cake layers, cooled
    3½ cups (8 ounces) COOL WHIP
      Whipped Topping, thawed

DISSOLVE gelatin in boiling water. Add pineapple and ice cubes. Stir until gelatin begins to thicken, 3 to 5 minutes. Remove any unmelted ice. Chill until thickened.

SPOON 1 cup thickened gelatin over each cake layer; chill about 15 minutes.

FOLD whipped topping into remaining gelatin mixture. (If mixture becomes too thick, add milk until frosting is of desired consistency.)

PLACE 1 cake layer, gelatin side up, on serving plate. Top with second cake layer, gelatin side up. Frost sides and about 1 inch around top edge of cake with whipped topping mixture. Chill until ready to serve.   *MAKES 12 servings*

Prep time: 30 minutes
Chill time: 1 hour

Clockwise from top: Happy Birthday Dessert; Pineapple Party Cake; Butterfly Cupcakes (page 67)

Fun for Children

Gelatin Tilt

1 package (4-serving size)
    JELL-O Brand Gelatin, any
    flavor
COOL WHIP Whipped
    Topping, thawed
    (optional)
JELL-O Jigglers (see page 83
    for recipe) (optional)

PREPARE gelatin as directed on
package. Measure ⅔ cup gelatin
into small bowl; chill until slightly
thickened. Pour remaining gelatin
into parfait or any stemmed glasses,
filling each glass about ½ full. Tilt
glasses in refrigerator by catching
bases of glasses between bars of
refrigerator rack and leaning tops
of glasses against wall. Chill until
set but not firm.

WHIP reserved gelatin at high
speed of electric mixer until fluffy
and thick. Spoon lightly over set
gelatin in glasses. Chill upright
until set, about 2 hours. Garnish
with whipped topping and JELL-O
Jigglers, if desired.

MAKES 4 servings

Prep time: 20 minutes
Chill time: 2 hours

Microwave Popcorn Balls

¼ cup (½ stick) PARKAY
    Margarine
1 bag (10½ ounces) KRAFT
    Miniature Marshmallows
1 package (4-serving size)
    JELL-O Brand Gelatin, any
    flavor
12 cups popped popcorn
1 cup peanuts (optional)

COMBINE margarine and
marshmallows in large
microwavable bowl. Microwave on
HIGH 1½ to 2 minutes or until
marshmallows are puffed. Add
gelatin; stir until well blended.
Pour marshmallow mixture over
combined popcorn and peanuts.
Stir to coat well. Shape into balls or
other shapes with greased hands.

*MAKES about 2 dozen
popcorn balls*

Prep time: 10 minutes

*Clockwise from top left: Gelatin Tilt;
JELL-O Jigglers (page 83); Pitcher's
Mounds (page 72); Microwave
Popcorn Balls; "Out of the Park"
Pudding-Wiches (page 72)*

Pitcher's Mounds

1 package (4-serving size)
   JELL-O Instant Pudding
   and Pie Filling, Chocolate
   Flavor
2 cups cold milk
3½ cups (8 ounces) COOL WHIP
   Whipped Topping, thawed
1 package (16 ounces)
   chocolate sandwich
   cookies, crushed
8 to 10 (8-ounce) paper or
   plastic cups

PREPARE pudding mix with milk
as directed on package. Let stand 5
minutes. Fold in whipped topping
and ½ of the crushed cookies.

PLACE about 1 tablespoon crushed
cookies in each cup. Fill cups
about ¾ full with pudding
mixture. Top with remaining
crushed cookies. Chill until set,
about 1 hour. Place toy sports
figure in center of each "mound,"
if desired.

MAKES 8 to 10 servings

Prep time: 15 minutes
Chill time: 1 hour

"Out of the Park" Pudding-Wiches

½ cup peanut butter
1½ cups cold milk
1 package (4-serving size)
   JELL-O Instant Pudding
   and Pie Filling, any flavor
Assorted cookies
Sprinkles (optional)

STIR peanut butter in small bowl
until smooth. Gradually stir in
milk. Add pudding mix. Beat with
wire whisk or at low speed of
electric mixer until well blended,
1 to 2 minutes.

SPREAD pudding mixture about
½ inch thick on cookie. Top with
second cookie, pressing cookies
together lightly and smoothing
edges of pudding mixture with
spatula. Coat edges with sprinkles,
if desired. Repeat making
sandwiches with remaining cookies
and filling. Freeze until firm, about
3 hours.

*MAKES about 2 dozen
pudding-wiches*

Note: Pudding-wiches can be
wrapped and stored in freezer up
to 2 weeks.

Prep time: 15 minutes
Freezing time: 3 hours

Fruity Dip

Fruity Dip

Kids love to dip food. They will have lots of fun dipping cookies, fruit or even fingers into this delicious treat.

1 package (8 ounces)
    PHILADELPHIA BRAND
    Cream Cheese, softened
1 package (4-serving size)
    JELL-O Brand Gelatin, any
    flavor
¼ cup milk
    Assorted fruit and cookies*

STIR cream cheese in small bowl until smooth. Gradually stir in gelatin and milk until well blended. Chill until ready to serve. Let stand at room temperature to soften slightly, if necessary. Garnish with fruit, if desired. Serve with fruit and cookies.

MAKES 1½ cups

*We suggest sliced apples or pears, grapes or strawberries.

Prep time: 5 minutes

Chocolate-Cherry Sundaes

A layered dessert that combines two kids' favorites, cherry gelatin and chocolate ice cream.

**1 package (4-serving size) JELL-O Brand Gelatin, Cherry Flavor
1 cup boiling water
½ cup cold water
1 cup chocolate ice cream, softened
COOL WHIP Whipped Topping, thawed
Chocolate syrup
Maraschino cherries (optional)**

DISSOLVE gelatin in boiling water. Measure ½ cup of the gelatin into small bowl. Add cold water; set aside. Spoon ice cream into remaining gelatin, stirring until melted and smooth. Spoon into individual dessert dishes. Chill until set but not firm, about 10 minutes.

SPOON reserved gelatin over creamy layer in dishes. Chill until set, about 1 hour. Top each dessert with dollop of whipped topping; drizzle with chocolate syrup. Garnish with cherry, if desired.

MAKES 6 servings

Prep time: 15 minutes
Chill time: 1 hour

Ice Cream Cone Cakes

Kids will love these "cupcakes" and you will love the fact that pudding is in the frosting.

**1 package (2-layer size) yellow cake mix
24 flat-bottom ice cream cones
Fluffy Pudding Frosting (recipe follows)
Sprinkles (optional)**

PREPARE cake mix as directed on package. Spoon about ¼ cup batter into each cone. Set cones on baking sheet. Bake at 350° for 25 minutes. Cool on rack. Spoon Fluffy Pudding Frosting over cakes; garnish with sprinkles, if desired.

MAKES 2 dozen cones

Fluffy Pudding Frosting

**1 cup cold milk
1 package (4-serving size) JELL-O Instant Pudding and Pie Filling, any flavor
¼ cup confectioners sugar (optional)
3½ cups (8 ounces) COOL WHIP Whipped Topping, thawed**

POUR milk into large bowl. Add pudding mix and sugar. Beat with wire whisk until well blended, 1 to 2 minutes. Fold in whipped topping. Spread on cakes immediately.

MAKES about 4 cups

Note: Store frosted cakes in refrigerator.

Prep time: 15 minutes
Baking time: 25 minutes

Clockwise from top right: Chocolate-Cherry Sundaes; Ice Cream Cone Cakes; Gelatin Sundaes (page 76)

Gelatin Sundaes

1 package (4-serving size)
   JELL-O Brand Gelatin,
   any flavor
¾ cup boiling water
½ cup cold water
   Ice cubes
1 pint ice cream, any flavor
1 cup thawed COOL WHIP
   Whipped Topping
¼ cup chopped nuts

DISSOLVE gelatin in boiling water.
Combine cold water and ice cubes
to make 1¼ cups. Add to gelatin,
stirring until slightly thickened.
Remove any unmelted ice.

SPOON ice cream and gelatin
alternately into tall sundae dishes,
ending with gelatin and filling to
within ½ inch of top of dish. Top
with whipped topping and nuts.
MAKES 4 servings

Prep time: 15 minutes

Sailboats

1 package (4-serving size)
   JELL-O Brand Gelatin, any
   flavor
1 can (8 ounces) peach slices,
   drained
½ cup banana slices
   Paper and wooden picks for
   sails

PREPARE gelatin as directed on
package. Chill until slightly
thickened. Reserve 8 peach slices
for garnish. Stir remaining peach
and banana slices into gelatin. Pour
into 4 individual dessert dishes.
Chill until firm, about 2 hours.

TOP gelatin with reserved peach
slices. Cut 4 small triangles from
paper to make sails (decorate sails
with crayons, if desired). Insert
wooden picks through sails; place
in gelatin.   *MAKES 4 servings*

Prep time: 20 minutes
Chill time: 2 hours

Funny Faces

These desserts, as much fun for
kids to make as they are to eat,
make a great activity for a party
or just a rainy day.

1 package (4-serving size)
   JELL-O Instant Pudding
   and Pie Filling, any flavor
2 cups cold milk
   BAKER'S ANGEL FLAKE
   Coconut*
   Popped popcorn
   Assorted candies and nuts
   Sprinkles

DECORATE individual dessert
dishes with paper cutouts, if
desired.

PREPARE pudding mix with milk
as directed on package. Let stand
5 minutes. Spoon pudding into
decorated dessert dishes. Make
faces on pudding with coconut,
popcorn, candies, nuts and
sprinkles. Chill until ready to
serve.   *MAKES 4 servings*

*Coconut may be tinted, if desired
(see page 10 for directions).

Prep time: 20 minutes

Funny Faces

Merry-Go-Round Cake

This makes an ordinary cake into a carousel of fun.

1 package (6-serving size)
JELL-O Instant Pudding
and Pie Filling, Vanilla
Flavor
1 package (2-layer size)
yellow cake mix
4 eggs
1 cup water
¼ cup vegetable oil
⅓ cup BAKER'S Semi-Sweet
Real Chocolate Chips,
melted
⅔ cup cold milk
Sprinkles (optional)
Paper carousel roof
(directions follow)
3 plastic straws
6 animal crackers

RESERVE ⅓ cup pudding mix.
Combine cake mix, remaining
pudding mix, eggs, water and oil in
large bowl. Beat at low speed of
electric mixer just to moisten,
scraping sides of bowl often. Beat
at medium speed 4 minutes. Pour
½ of the batter into greased and
floured 10-inch fluted tube pan.
Mix chocolate into remaining
batter. Spoon over batter in pan;
cut through with spatula in zigzag
pattern to marbleize. Bake at 350°
for 50 minutes or until cake tester
inserted in center comes out clean.
Cool in pan 15 minutes. Remove
from pan; finish cooling on rack.

BEAT reserved pudding mix and
milk in small bowl until smooth.
Spoon over top of cake to glaze.
Garnish with sprinkles, if desired.

Merry-Go-Round Cake

CUT 10- to 12-inch circle from
colored paper; scallop edges, if
desired. Make 1 slit to center
(Diagram 1). Overlap cut edges to
form carousel roof; secure with
tape (Diagram 2). Cut straws in
half; arrange on cake with animal
crackers. Top with roof.

MAKES 12 servings

Prep time: 30 minutes
Baking time: 50 minutes

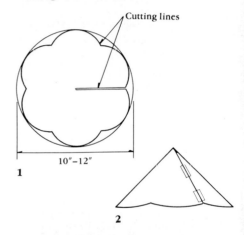

Carousel Gelatin Cups

1 package (4-serving size)
JELL-O Brand Gelatin, any
red flavor
Teddy bear cookies or
animal crackers
COOL WHIP Whipped
Topping, thawed

PREPARE gelatin as directed on
package. Pour into individual
serving dishes. Chill until firm,
about 2 hours. Arrange cookies
around inside rim of each dish.
Garnish with whipped topping.

MAKES 4 servings

Prep time: 10 minutes
Chill time: 2 hours

Chocolate Peanut Butter Cups

¾ cup chocolate cookie crumbs
3 tablespoons PARKAY
    Margarine, melted
½ cup peanut butter
1 cup cold milk
1 package (4-serving size)
    JELL-O Instant Pudding
    and Pie Filling, Chocolate
    Flavor
2 cups thawed COOL WHIP
    Whipped Topping
    Chocolate topping*

LINE 12 muffin cups with paper baking cups. Mix together cookie crumbs and margarine in small bowl. Press about 1 tablespoon crumb mixture onto bottom of each cup.

STIR peanut butter in small bowl until smooth. Gradually stir in milk. Add pudding mix. Beat with wire whisk or at low speed of electric mixer until well blended, 1 to 2 minutes. Fold in whipped topping. Spoon mixture into cups. Freeze 3 hours or overnight. Peel off paper just before serving. Drizzle chocolate topping over each cup.

MAKES 1 dozen cups

*Use commercial topping that forms hard coating on ice cream.

Vanilla Peanut Butter Cups:
Prepare Chocolate Peanut Butter Cups as directed, substituting graham cracker crumbs for chocolate cookie crumbs and vanilla flavor pudding for chocolate flavor pudding. Top each cup with 1 teaspoon strawberry preserves in place of chocolate topping.

Prep time: 10 minutes
Freezing time: 3 hours

Peanut Butter and Jelly Cake-Wiches

½ cup peanut butter
1¼ cups cold milk
1 package (4-serving size)
    JELL-O Instant Pudding
    and Pie Filling, Vanilla or
    Butterscotch Flavor
½ cup jelly or preserves
1 pound cake loaf (about
    12 ounces), cut into 16
    slices
    Chocolate Drizzle (see page
    15 for directions)

STIR peanut butter in small bowl until smooth. Gradually stir in milk. Add pudding mix. Beat with wire whisk or at low speed of electric mixer until well blended, 1 to 2 minutes. Chill 15 minutes.

SPREAD jelly thinly over ½ of the cake slices. Spread remaining cake slices with pudding mixture. Prepare sandwiches with cake slices. Chill. Cut into shapes; decorate with Chocolate Drizzle.

MAKES about 1½ dozen cake-wiches

Prep time: 20 minutes

These recipes take a universal kid favorite — peanut butter — and make it into delicious treats for any party or get-together.

Clockwise from top left: Chocolate Peanut Butter Cups; Peanut Butter and Jelly Cake-Wiches; Vanilla Peanut Butter Cups

JELL-O Jiggler gelatin snacks in all colors and shapes! Following is a fun assortment of JELL-O Jiggler recipes guaranteed to put a smile on any child's face.

JELL-O Creamy Jigglers
Gelatin Snacks

2½ cups boiling water or boiling fruit juice
4 packages (4-serving size each) or 2 packages (8-serving size each) JELL-O Brand Gelatin, any flavor
1 cup cold milk
1 package (4-serving size) JELL-O Instant Pudding and Pie Filling, Vanilla Flavor

ADD boiling water to gelatin. Dissolve completely; cool to room temperature.

POUR milk into small bowl. Add pudding mix. Beat with wire whisk until well blended, 1 to 2 minutes. Quickly pour into gelatin. Stir with wire whisk until well blended. Pour into 13×9-inch pan. Chill until firm, about 3 hours.

DIP pan into warm water about 15 seconds for easy removal of JELL-O Jigglers. Use cookie cutters to cut decorative shapes (umbrellas for showers, etc.). Remove from pan. Cut remaining gelatin into cubes.
MAKES about 3 dozen JELL-O Jigglers

Prep time: 15 minutes
Chill time: 3 hours

JELL-O Jigglers

JELL-O Jigglers
Gelatin Snacks

2½ cups boiling water or boiling fruit juice
4 packages (4-serving size each) or 2 packages (8-serving size each) JELL-O Brand Gelatin, any flavor

ADD boiling water to gelatin. Dissolve completely. Pour into 13×9-inch pan. Chill until firm, about 3 hours.

DIP pan in warm water about 15 seconds for easy removal of JELL-O Jigglers. Use cookie cutters to cut decorative shapes in gelatin (hearts for Valentine's Day, pumpkins for Halloween, stars for sports parties, etc.). Remove from pan. Cut remaining gelatin into cubes.
MAKES about 3 dozen JELL-O Jigglers

Notes: For thicker JELL-O Jigglers, use 8- or 9-inch square pan.

To use ice cube trays or JELL-O Jiggler molds, pour dissolved gelatin into 2 or 3 ice cube trays. Chill until firm, about 2 hours. To remove, dip trays in warm water about 15 seconds. Moisten tips of fingers; gently pull from edges and remove from trays.

Prep time: 10 minutes
Chill time: 3 hours

JELL-O Jiggler Surprises
Gelatin Snacks

2½ cups boiling water or boiling
    fruit juice
  4 packages (4-serving size
    each) or 2 packages
    (8-serving size each)
    JELL-O Brand Gelatin,
    any flavor
    Banana slices
    Strawberry slices
    Canned pineapple slices, cut
    into bite-size pieces

ADD boiling water to gelatin.
Dissolve completely. Pour into
13×9-inch pan. Arrange fruit in
gelatin so that when cut into
decorative shapes, each will
contain 1 piece of fruit. Chill until
firm, about 3 hours.

DIP pan in warm water about 15
seconds for easy removal of JELL-O
Jigglers. Use cookie cutters to cut
gelatin into decorative shapes.
Remove from pan. Cut remaining
gelatin into cubes.

MAKES about 3 dozen
JELL-O Jigglers

Prep time: 10 minutes
Chill time: 3 hours

JELL-O Tropical Jigglers
Gelatin Snacks

2½ cups boiling water or boiling
    fruit juice
  4 packages (4-serving size
    each) or 2 packages
    (8-serving size each)
    JELL-O Brand Gelatin,
    Strawberry-Banana or
    Orange Flavor
  1 can (8 ounces) crushed
    pineapple in juice,
    undrained

ADD boiling water to gelatin.
Dissolve completely. Stir in
pineapple. Pour into 13×9-inch
pan. Chill until firm, about 3
hours.

DIP pan in warm water about 15
seconds for easy removal of JELL-O
Jigglers. Use cookie cutters to cut
decorative shapes in gelatin.
Remove from pan. Cut remaining
gelatin into cubes.

MAKES about 3 dozen
JELL-O Jigglers

JELL-O Vegetable Jigglers: Use
lemon, lime or orange flavor
gelatin. Omit pineapple. Stir in
½ cup each shredded carrot, finely
chopped celery and finely chopped
cucumber and 3 tablespoons
vinegar.

Prep time: 10 minutes
Chill time: 3 hours

JELL-O Jigglers (page 83); JELL-O
Jiggler Surprises; JELL-O Tropical
Jigglers; JELL-O Creamy Jigglers (page
83); JELL-O Vegetable Jigglers

Delicious Drinks

Cranberry-Orange Cooler

A nice alternative to iced tea. Just as refreshing, but prettier.

1 package (4-serving size)
    JELL-O Brand Gelatin,
    Orange Flavor
1 cup boiling water
2½ cups cranberry juice,
    chilled
    Ice cubes (optional)
    Orange slices (optional)

DISSOLVE gelatin in boiling water. Add cranberry juice. Pour over ice cubes in tall glasses and garnish with orange slices, if desired.

MAKES about 3½ cups or 4 servings

Prep time: 5 minutes

Several of the recipes in this chapter call for alcohol as an ingredient. We urge you to use them responsibly. Remember, drinking and driving don't mix.

Lime Party Punch

1 package (4-serving size)
    JELL-O Brand Gelatin, Lime
    Flavor
1 package (4-serving size)
    JELL-O Brand Gelatin,
    Lemon Flavor
2 cups boiling water
1 bottle (1 liter) club soda,
    lemon soda or lemon-lime
    carbonated beverage,
    chilled
1 cup white wine (optional)
1 orange, lemon or lime,
    thinly sliced
    Ice cubes (optional)

DISSOLVE gelatins in boiling water; cool. (Keep at room temperature until ready to serve.) Stir in club soda, wine and orange slices just before serving. Serve over ice, if desired.

MAKES 8 cups or 16 servings

Prep time: 10 minutes

Clockwise from left: Cranberry-Orange Cooler; Lime Party Punch; Strawberry-Ginger Punch (page 92)

Easy Eggnog

2 packages (4-serving size
  each) JELL-O Instant
  Pudding and Pie Filling,
  French Vanilla or Vanilla
  Flavor
2 quarts cold milk
2 quarts cold prepared eggnog
1 cup brandy, rum or orange
  liqueur

COMBINE pudding mix with 2
cups of the milk; stir until slightly
thickened. Stir in remaining 6 cups
milk and eggnog until well
blended. Stir in brandy. Chill until
ready to serve. Top with whipped
topping and sprinkle with nutmeg,
if desired.

*MAKES about 18 cups
or 36 servings*

Prep time: 10 minutes

Nonalcoholic Gelatin Shots

*Gelatin shots began as a fad
several years ago, becoming a
popular order in the bar scene.
They are usually served in small
paper cups and eaten like Italian
ices. Try the combinations here,
or create some of your own.*

1 package (4-serving size)
  JELL-O Brand Gelatin, any
  flavor
1 cup boiling water
1 cup cold liquid (see
  variations below)

DISSOLVE gelatin in boiling water.
Add cold liquid. Pour into 12
(2-ounce) souffle cups. Chill until
set, about 1 hour.

MAKES 12 servings

Cherry Cola Shots: Use cherry
flavor gelatin and cola beverage.

Creamy Orange Shots: Use orange
flavor gelatin. Substitute 1 cup
vanilla ice cream for cold liquid.

Gingerberry Shots: Use raspberry
or strawberry flavor gelatin and
ginger ale.

Tangy Peach Shots: Use peach
flavor gelatin. Substitute 1
container (8 ounces) peach or
vanilla yogurt for cold liquid.

Sunshine Shots: Dissolve 1
package (4-serving size) orange
flavor gelatin in 1 cup boiling
water; add 1 cup cold sparkling
water. Repeat with 1 package
(4-serving size) strawberry flavor
gelatin. Pour orange gelatin into 24
(2-ounce) souffle cups, filling each
cup halfway. Chill until almost set,
about 20 minutes. Pour strawberry
gelatin over orange gelatin in cups.
Chill until set, about 1 hour. Makes
24 servings.

Prep time: 10 minutes
Chill time: 1 hour

Nonalcoholic Gelatin Shots (page 88) and "Light" Gelatin Shots

"Light" Gelatin Shots

    **1 package (4-serving size)
JELL-O Brand Gelatin, any
flavor
1 cup boiling water
¾ cup cold juice or soda
¼ cup cold liqueur, rum or
wine**

DISSOLVE gelatin in boiling water.
Add juice and liqueur. Pour into 12
(2-ounce) souffle cups. Chill until
set, about 1 hour.

               MAKES 12 servings

Cherry-Rum Cola Shots: Use
cherry flavor gelatin, ¾ cup cola
beverage and ¼ cup rum.

Orange Triplex: Use orange flavor
gelatin, ¾ cup orange flavor
sparkling water and ¼ cup any
orange liqueur.

Prep time: 10 minutes
Chill time: 1 hour

Frosty Pudding Milk Shakes

The best of both worlds—a creamy milk shake with the taste of an ice cream soda.

> 2 cups cold milk
> 1 package (4-serving size) JELL-O Instant Pudding and Pie Filling, any flavor
> 1 pint ice cream, any flavor
> Club soda

POUR milk into blender. Add pudding mix and ice cream; cover. Blend at high speed 30 seconds. Scrape sides of container; blend 30 seconds longer. Pour into glasses. Top with club soda. Serve immediately.

> *MAKES about 5 cups or 4 to 6 servings*

Prep time: 5 minutes

Easy Pudding Milk Shakes

Pudding mix makes these milk shakes extra thick and creamy.

> 3 cups cold milk
> 1 package (4-serving size) JELL-O Instant Pudding and Pie Filling, any flavor
> 1½ cups ice cream, any flavor

POUR milk into blender. Add pudding mix and ice cream; cover. Blend at high speed 30 seconds or until smooth. Pour into glasses. Serve immediately. (Mixture thickens as it stands. Thin with additional milk, if desired.)

> *MAKES about 5 cups or 4 to 6 servings*

Prep time: 5 minutes

Fruit Flavor Milk Shakes

Kids will love the different colors and flavors!

> 2 cups cold milk
> 1 package (4-serving size) JELL-O Brand Gelatin, any flavor
> 1 pint vanilla ice cream

POUR milk into blender. Add gelatin and ice cream; cover. Blend at high speed 30 seconds or until smooth. Pour into glasses.

> *MAKES about 4 cups or 4 servings*

Prep time: 5 minutes

Clockwise from top: Fruit Flavor Milk Shakes; Frosty Pudding Milk Shakes; Easy Pudding Milk Shakes

Strawberry Ginger Punch

This recipe is easy, delicious and great for a crowd. The strawberry and ginger ale flavor combination is irresistible.

> 1 package (4-serving size) JELL-O Brand Gelatin, Strawberry Flavor
> ¼ cup sugar
> 1½ cups boiling water
> 2½ cups cold water
> 1 package (10 ounces) BIRDS EYE Quick Thaw Strawberries
> 1 can (6 ounces) frozen concentrated lemonade or limeade
> 1 bottle (1 liter) ginger ale, chilled
> Mint leaves
> Ice cubes (optional)

DISSOLVE gelatin and sugar in boiling water. Add cold water, strawberries and concentrate; stir until strawberries and concentrate are thawed. Chill until ready to serve. Stir in ginger ale and mint. Serve over ice, if desired.

MAKES 10 cups or 20 servings

Prep time: 10 minutes

"Glogg"

This hot beverage and a roaring fire will warm up any cold day.

> 1 package (4-serving size) JELL-O Brand Gelatin, any flavor
> 3 cups boiling water
> 1 cinnamon stick
> 6 whole cloves
> 3 orange slices

DISSOLVE gelatin in boiling water in 4-cup measuring cup. Add cinnamon stick, cloves and orange slices. Cover; let stand 5 minutes. Remove spices and oranges. Pour gelatin mixture into mugs; serve warm. Garnish with additional cinnamon sticks and clove-studded orange slices, if desired.

MAKES about 3 cups or 4 to 6 servings

Prep time: 5 minutes

Microwave Hot Chocolate

> 4 cups milk
> 1 package (4-serving size) JELL-O Pudding and Pie Filling, Chocolate or Chocolate Fudge Flavor
> COOL WHIP Whipped Topping, thawed (optional)
> Chocolate Curls (see page 14 for directions) (optional)

POUR milk into 2-quart microwavable bowl. Add pudding mix. Beat with wire whisk until well blended. Microwave on HIGH 5 minutes; whisk again. Pour into mugs. Top with whipped topping and garnish with Chocolate Curls, if desired.

MAKES about 4 cups or 4 servings

Prep time: 5 minutes
Cooking time: 5 minutes

Top: "Glogg;" bottom: Microwave Hot Chocolate

Index

METRIC CONVERSION CHART

VOLUME MEASUREMENTS (dry)

⅛ teaspoon = 0.5 mL

¼ teaspoon = 1 mL

½ teaspoon = 2 mL

¾ teaspoon = 4 mL

1 teaspoon = 5 mL

1 tablespoon = 15 mL

2 tablespoons = 30 mL

¼ cup = 60 mL

⅓ cup = 75 mL

½ cup = 125 mL

⅔ cup = 150 mL

¼ cup = 175 mL

1 cup = 250 mL

2 cups = 1 pint = 500 mL

3 cups = 750 mL

4 cups = 1 quart = 1 L

VOLUME MEASUREMENTS (fluid)

1 fluid ounce (2 tablespoons) = 30 mL

4 fluid ounces (½ cup) = 125 mL

8 fluid ounces (1 cup) = 250 mL

12 fluid ounces (1½ cups) = 375 mL

16 fluid ounces (2 cups) = 500 mL

WEIGHTS (mass)

½ ounce = 15 g

1 ounce = 30 g

3 ounces = 90 g

4 ounces = 120 g

8 ounces = 225 g

10 ounces = 285 g

12 ounces = 360 g

16 ounces = 1 pound = 450 g

DIMENSIONS

1/16 inch = 2 mm

⅛ inch = 3 mm

¼ inch = 6 mm

½ inch = 1.5 cm

¾ inch = 2 cm

1 inch = 2.5 cm

OVEN TEMPERATURES

250°F = 120°C

275°F = 140°C

300°F = 150°C

325°F = 160°C

350°F = 180°C

375°F = 190°C

400°F = 200°C

425°F = 220°C

450°F = 230°C

BAKING PAN SIZES

Utensil	Size in Inches/ Quarts	Metric Volume	Size in Centimeters
Baking or Cake Pan (square or rectangular)	8×8×2	2 L	20×20×5
	9×9×2	2.5 L	22×22×5
	12×8×2	3 L	30×20×5
	13×9×2	3.5 L	33×23×5
Loaf Pan	8×4×3	1.5 L	20×10×7
	9×5×3	2 L	23×13×7
Round Layer Cake Pan	8×1½	1.2 L	20×4
	9×1½	1.5 L	23×4
Pie Plate	8×1¼	750 mL	20×3
	9×1¼	1 L	23×3
Baking Dish or Casserole	1 quart	1 L	—
	1½ quart	1.5 L	—
	2 quart	2 L	—

Everyone loves JELL-O, and EASY ENTERTAINING contains both classic and creative new uses for JELL-O Brand Gelatin and Pudding! This captivating collection of over 80 dessert recipes is guaranteed to rekindle fond childhood memories and create delicious new traditions for today's generation of JELL-O lovers. Looking for an easy-to-make, no-fail, elegant dessert guaranteed to impress friends and family alike? Look no further . . . EASY ENTERTAINING has it all! No matter what the occasion—small impromptu gatherings, children's parties, or year-round holiday festivities—EASY ENTERTAINING promises sensational results every time!